PLACES TO GO WITH CHILDREN

AROUND PUGET SOUND

PLACES TO GO WITH CHILDREN AROUND
Puget Sound

ELTON WELKE

Completely Revised and Expanded

THIRD EDITION

CHRONICLE BOOKS
SAN FRANCISCO

Printed in the United States of America.

Third Edition

Library of Congress Cataloging in Publication Data
Welke, Elton.
    Places to go with children around Puget Sound / Elton Welke. —
3rd ed.
        p.   cm.
    Includes index.
    ISBN 0-8118-0635-9
    1. Puget Sound Region (Wash.)—Guidebooks.   2. Family recre-
ation—Washington (State)—Puget Sound Region—Guidebooks.
3. Outdoor recreation—Washington (State)—Puget Sound Region—
Guidebooks.   4. Children—Travel—Washington (State)—Puget Sound
Region—Guidebooks.
F897.P9W45   1994
917.97'70443—dc20   93-34854
                                                CIP

Design and illustration: Karen Smidth
Composition: Words & Deeds

Distributed in Canada by Raincoast Books, 112 East Third Ave.,
Vancouver, B.C. V5T 1C8

10 9 8 7 6 5 4 3 2 1

Chronicle Books
275 Fifth Street
San Francisco, CA 94103

Contents

To Allison, Erik, Erin, Spencer, and Lian

Preface to Third Edition

Seven-year old Erin Irene became an aunt this year with the arrival of grandson Spencer, now one year old as this edition goes to press. He has recharged the subject of things to do and places to go with children, while Aunt Erin has continued to serve as expert and technical editor. She also remains the number-one fan of Seattle's Woodland Park Zoo, a devotee of Puget Sound beaches, and a tenacious raspberry picker.

To the several loyal, if critical, readers who have been in touch as information in the previous edition became dated and obsolete, my sincere thanks. We do indeed acknowledge the *new* Seattle Art Museum in this edition, and in keeping with the times we note that Archie McPhee's now features a latte bar! My heartfelt thanks to Karin Gallagher, researcher and harvester par excellence, who nurtured this text into the electronic age; to friend and colleague Tony Dirksen for his thoughtful ways and suggestions over many years; and once again to Bonnie Lum Welke for the hours of fact checking, suggestions, field work, and expertise as a mom. And a very special thanks to Bill LeBlond, an editor who combines the doggedness of Captain Ahab with the patience of Job and the wisdom of Solomon.

Preface to Second Edition

If the Man Who Has Everything were a kid, he'd want to live in Seattle. Since *Places to Go with Children Around Puget Sound* was originally published in 1986, not only have the numbers and quality of activities for children in Seattle and around Puget Sound become even richer, but also Seattle has become an officially designated place for kids. In fact, at every major entrance to the city, signs proclaim "Seattle is a KidsPlace," underscoring the fact that while citizens of the Emerald City manage to tolerate the work ethic, they embrace recreation with boundless zeal and energy.

With more boats per capita than just about any place, snow skiing 45 minutes away, mountains and water in all directions, and parks—dozens and dozens of parks—well, Western Washington really is as much a playground as it is the business hub of the Pacific Northwest. The children's programs in Seattle, from theater to special events, are ongoing year round, and there are dozens of them.

In keeping with the spirit of KidsPlace, Erin Irene Welke, now age 3, officially joined the research team for the revision of *Places to Go with Children Around Puget Sound.* I'm grateful each and every day to her for keeping the subject energized...and for just being Erin. She performs both roles flawlessly.

Piping down the valleys wild,
Piping songs of pleasant glee,
On a cloud I saw a child,
And he laughing said to me:
"Pipe a song about a Lamb!"
—WILLIAM BLAKE

Preface

The best place in the world to grow up is around Puget Sound. There are more things to do here, more adventures, more "goodies per mile" than any place else. In many ways the Puget Sound country is too sophisticated for adults, but it is a wondrous region, perfectly suited for children. And the best possible way for an adult to explore it is with a child as a guide.

In 20 years of wandering and writing about Western Washington for *Sunset Magazine, Better Homes and Gardens,* and other publications, I've never tired of watching children discover the mysteries of Puget Sound. I've watched my own son and daughter shuck their first oysters, catch their first fish, stalk the not-so-elusive wild huckleberry, and literally soak their feet in natural history in the foothills of Western Washington. They live in California now, but their tap roots are here.

This book is a reminder for them to look back on and for all of us to look forward to. I strongly believe that the best places to explore with children are the places you enjoy yourself. If you like to ride ferry boats, visit hands-on museums, wade in tidepools, catch fish, collect rocks, see wild animals, pet rabbits, climb around old forts, gather berries, stalk geoducks, sail small boats, and enjoy all the wonderful things life offers when you have sand in your shoes, Puget Sound is for you.

Regional guides are usually organized by geography; this guide is organized by activities. Although the area is large and diverse, no place mentioned in this book is more than a day's outing, round trip. Most of the public parks selected are "free" for day use as described. However, fees may be charged for overnight camping, and reservations are often required for weekend camping. I have provided telephone numbers so that readers may obtain up-to-date information. All are in area code 206.

I owe thanks to many colleagues over many years for their contributions herein. A special, heartfelt thank you goes to Don Normark and Doug Wilson. And my grateful acknowledgment to Bonnie Lum Welke, who drifted into this project as a volunteer editorial assistant and completed the book as its senior editor.

Introduction

EQUIPPING EXPEDITIONS

The biggest kid I know is a 50-year-old Seattle physician. He is a regular patron of the ballet, repertory theater, gallery openings, and the best restaurants in town. He is also as compulsively drawn to water as, say, your typical Labrador retriever.

He romps around tide flats, falls off logs into beaver ponds, sloshes through streams and creeks, and will instinctively take the wettest course across any given street on a rainy day. He travels with a dozen fishing rods, a clamming shovel, and a crayfish trap in his car at all times, and he's been known to arrive an hour late if the route to his destination took him past an oyster beach at low tide.

Along with the sporting goods inventory he packs in the back of his four-wheel-drive clam-attack vehicle, he always carries a *complete change of clothing.* What works for this big kid is appropriate for children of all ages, and it makes the difference between youngsters and parents enjoying an adventure together and enduring a day-long marathon of chronic complaints and runny noses.

On every outing (including school outings) carry a dry change of clothing for everyone, and be sure to include extra socks, shoes or boots, and a spare jacket or sweater. It does rain occasionally in the Puget Sound region, and most youngsters worth their salt water will get their feet wet at every opportunity.

Full tummies are also important to small armies, especially in cool weather. Wise parents often carry snacks (trail mix, granola bars, carrot sticks, cookies, fresh fruit, sandwiches) or plan trips that will not take them far from commercial food sources. Although not famous for gourmet burgers, the Washington State ferries serve snacks and meals. A cup of hot chocolate makes a nice break during ferry crossings.

Few of us have the abundant energy of my water-loving doctor friend, but think about carrying a few of the items that work for him when traveling through the Puget Sound region. Consider the frustration of driving along Hood Canal at low tide and seeing what appears to be everyone in the world gathering clams except you and your family. With a bucket and small shovel you can take advantage of these opportunities. With a copy of local tide tables you can plan these opportunities!

These are only suggestions; you wouldn't or couldn't pack everything all the time:

- Complete change of clothing for everyone
- Rain gear
- Good road map
- Puget Sound nautical chart
- Tide tables
- Ferry schedule
- Small shovels/buckets for clamming
- Oyster-shucking knife
- Medium/lightweight spinning rods and reels (with bait hooks/ assorted lures)
- Crayfish trap
- Binoculars
- Snacks
- Natural history field guides

It wasn't too long ago that field guides to wildlife identification were either too generalized or poorly illustrated to use. Happily, this has changed and there are now many excellent new guides to birds, seashore life, and other critters, some of them local to the Puget Sound region and/ or the Far West. You'll find field guides for most interests at libraries and for sale in comprehensive bookstores.

1
Animal Watching

Zoos, aquariums, and big game parks offer animal watching year round. Public parks and many bays and tide flats throughout the Puget Sound region provide extraordinary bird watching, especially in the spring and fall when great flights of migratory waterfowl and shorebirds make their annual journeys North and South.

Though not a necessity, a good bird guide helps to identify species, and older children enjoy using the colorful books to "key" the birds they see. Thanks to the Japanese optical industry, inexpensive binoculars are readily available. The standard binocular power for bird watching is 7 x 35 or 7 x 50 (the first number, 7, is power of magnification; the second number, often 35 or 50, is the diameter of the outside lens opening in millimeters, which determines the light-gathering power). Less powerful binoculars, even 3 x 20 opera glasses, are fine. Avoid high-powered binoculars in the 10 x 50 category. They are heavy and blurry to look through unless tripod-mounted for steadiness.

Though the practice is probably not approved by the National Audubon Society, younger children always enjoy feeding ducks, and around Puget Sound you are never far from ducks to feed. Dry-bread leftovers are the standard duck food. Cookies are not recommended, although, if the truth be told, an occasional Oreo may at times be sacrificed in the interest of good feathered public relations. One caution, however, is the growing concern of some city councils about feeding and attracting waterfowl in public areas. Health issues are usually cited as the reason for prohibitions, but birds can be messy in any event. City elders like their wildlife neat and tidy.

Salmon runs occur at many different times, but the predictably active period is autumn—from mid-August through mid-November—the best time to visit salmon hatcheries.

Early summer is the best time to watch the large numbers of deer feeding on fresh new grasses in meadows of the Cascade and Olympic mountains.

✴ Woodland Park Zoo

5500 Phinney N., Seattle. 684-4800. Daily, 9:30–4; 9:30–6, summer.
Adults $6; youths (6–17) $3.50; children (5 and under) free.

An outstanding zoo, and getting better by the day. Small children love the family farm where they can pet some of the animals. Everyone loves the African savanna where lions, zebras, giraffes, springboks, and a host of other animals wander freely. Monkeys and elephants cavort in tropical forests, exotic birds preen and flutter everywhere. The nocturnal house provides a fascinating look into the way many secretive animals live their nighttime lives while the rest of us sleep. "The nightlife is wild," reports one of the zoo's delightful promotion pieces that pictures a furry little lemur with huge green eyes.

The recently opened Tropical Rain Forest is an extraordinary addition, with poison dart frogs, the world's smallest monkeys, free-flying birds, and lowland gorillas. Scheduled for debut soon are a Temperate Forest exhibit and the Northern Trail, a habitat for bald eagles, brown bears, and river otters.

Easily, this is the best zoo in the Pacific Northwest. Rules are few and sensible: Stay on paths, don't feed the animals, and leave your own pets at home.

✴ Seattle Aquarium

Pier 59, Waterfront Park, Seattle. 386-4320. Daily, 10–5, winter;
10–7, summer. Adults $6.50; youths (13–18) and Seniors $5; children
(6–12) $1.50.

Much is made of the Seattle Aquarium's educational virtues, and rightly so. It is a superb place to learn about the natural history of Puget Sound and Puget Sound's marine life, with extraordinary displays of fish and marine mammals. It's also a lot of fun.

Children may actually pick up tide-pool creatures in a hands-on tide-pool exhibit and Discovery Lab. In a walk-through exhibit area designed to bring people and marine mammals together, you can watch seals and sea otters play for the audience and each other in sometimes lightning-fast movements that are pure aquatic ballet.

If the weather is chilly, bundle up for the aquarium. Temperatures are maintained for the comfort of the resident critters, not visitors. And some of the exhibits are open air.

The aquarium has an active and varied schedule of programs for the entire family, including cruises on a research ship around Elliott Bay, cruising or kayaking in the San Juan Islands, and whale watching. Cruises are popular, so make reservations well in advance.

✻ Point Defiance Park

N. 45th and Pearl, Tacoma. 591-5341. Aquarium and zoo open daily, 9–dusk.

There are many good reasons to visit Point Defiance Park (see Chapters 5 and 10), but the aquarium/zoo complex heads the list. Animals, including otters, walruses, and polar bears, are observed in natural habitats. There is a bat cave exhibit that may disquiet the squeamish but that fascinates children. The aquarium is strong on local sea life.

With recent remodeling activity and renewed interest from the community, this zoo facility is really coming into its own.

✻ Hurricane Ridge

Olympic National Park, 17 miles south of Port Angeles off U.S. Highway 101. 452-0329 for weather. Mid- and late summer. Free.

Hurricane Ridge, at an elevation of 5,200 feet, is in the heart of the Olympic Mountains and one of the most popular destinations in Olympic National Park. From Hurricane you look across the canyons into the very soul of the mountains.

Hurricane Ridge is famous for its deer, and in July—springtime here—you walk through flowery meadows where deer step nonchalantly along your path. A large number of wild deer appear here to feed on fresh mountain grasses, and your chance of sighting these lovely animals is about as certain as anything in the wilderness can be.

In July and August there is a sense of perpetual celebration in the Olympics. Within yards of trailheads marmots scurry from rock to rock, insects hum in the wildflowers, mountain goats reign over the snowy ridgetops, and black-tailed deer graze belly-deep in avalanche lilies.

Pick a sunny day and bring a picnic lunch (stop at park headquarters in Port Angeles for a Hurricane Ridge weather report).

✻ Olympic Game Farm

1423 Ward Road, Sequim. 683-4295. Daily, 9–dusk, summer. Adults $4; Seniors $3; children (5–12) $3.

For 40 years this 180-acre preserve on the Olympic Peninsula has been home and training ground for film stars that have appeared in more than 70 motion pictures and a host of television commercials. You've seen them in *Never Cry Wolf* and the TV series "Grizzly Adams," and you may even recognize the bear that appeared in one of Ronald Reagan's much-discussed 1984 political advertisements.

More than 300 animals representing 40 species live here in outdoor fields and fenced compounds. You'll see a few exotics (Siberian tigers, zebras, leopards), but most of the animals are North American species—bison, bears, bobcats, foxes, wolves, even wolverines. Hand-raised from birth and trained to work with photographers and other actors, the animals are at ease around people.

Drive through the preserve to see most of the stars, but some are best seen on a guided lecture tour. Stars they may be, but some of the animals are accustomed to accepting handouts. Bread for feeding them is sold at the gate for 50 cents a loaf.

✳ Nisqually National Wildlife Refuge

Exit 114 from Interstate 5. 753-9467. Open daylight hours, year round. "Closed" signs are posted occasionally to protect the wildlife. $2 daily per family; free with federal Golden Eagle Pass.

The Nisqually Delta is a large and rare marsh habitat for more than 200 bird species, from resident songbirds to migratory waterfowl and shorebirds. Several trails take off from the parking area by the refuge office, ranging in length from five miles to a half-mile nature walk.

An observation deck at the environmental education center provides a sweeping view of marsh ponds and grasslands and skyscapes filled with bird life, and there is a second deck overlooking the wildlife-rich salt marsh. Binoculars greatly aid the bird watching, and serious students of ornithology often employ powerful telescopes or spotting scopes. A bird checklist is available at the refuge office.

In addition to bird life, there are 125 species of fish in the Nisqually Delta, along with some 50 other animals—from reptiles and amphibians to deer and otters.

✳ Dungeness National Wildlife Refuge

Exit Kitchen Road from U.S. Highway 101 just west of Sequim. 457-8451. $2 daily per family; free with federal Golden Eagle Pass.

This refuge occupies a portion of remarkable Dungeness Spit, a seven-and-one-half-mile long sand spit that juts out into the Strait of Juan de Fuca and serves as a resting place and home for an astonishing bird population, including perhaps the largest shorebird concentrations you'll see anywhere in the Northwest during spring and fall. Along with other geese and ducks, black brant also gather here in winter and spring.

The same rich beds of seaweed and shallow water edibles that attract the birds also attract a large crab population. There is good clam digging on the spit, and marine mammals—killer whales, sea lions, seals—are sometimes spotted here.

Dungeness is exposed to the vigorous winds that sometimes blow down the Strait of Juan de Fuca. Bring jackets for everyone in your expedition.

✯ Skagit Wildlife Recreation Area

Just southwest of Conway on the shores of Skagit Bay. Washington Department of Game. 682-6719. Free, unless you park on the reservation, in which case a $5 annual conservation license is required.

Except during hunting season (fall and early winter) this and other state wildlife recreation areas offer superb bird watching and the chance to see other wildlife, too. A $5 license (sold wherever fishing and hunting licenses are available) lets you drive on any of the state's wildlife recreation areas.

Skagit Bay and tidelands are rich in bird life, including great blue herons, cranes, pelicans, geese, and sea ducks. Wood ducks are seen in Big Ditch Slough, and bald eagles often soar here. During low tides the clamming is excellent, especially for eastern soft-shell clams.

In all, some 180 species of birds have been recorded in the area. The most dramatic appearances are by some 30,000 snow geese that move through the region from December to mid-April each year, and by several dozen rare whistling swans that winter on Skagit Bay. You may also see otter, muskrat, and beaver in the marshes and along the dikes.

✯ Marina Park

On Lake Washington, downtown Kirkland. Free.

The hungriest ducks and geese in all of Puget Sound reside in Kirkland City Park. The lively waterside park area has benches and grassy areas for picnicking. Several restaurants, delis, galleries, and shops are within easy walking distance, and their managements are at war with the ducks. Even the Kirkland City Council has joined the campaign against feeding waterfowl. Undaunted, the birds still congregate here.

The ducks are most numerous on the beach behind the parking area at the rear of Pelican Wharf. There's a good public fishing and boat-moorage pier here. In late winter and early spring the waterfowl, especially the colorful mallard ducks, display their courtship rituals—bobbing and dipping just off the beaches. Look for families with ducklings and goslings during April and May.

✯ Tumwater Falls Park

At Tumwater, just off Interstate 5 near Olympia. 943-2550. Daily, 8–dusk. Free.

This wonderful park features visible history, beautiful landscaping, picnic areas, a playground for toddlers, a mile of trail along the river, and salmon ladders where from late August through early September the king salmon runs are extraordinary.

A bit of background: Because of the height of Tumwater Falls, the upper Tumwater River did not have a native salmon population until a few years ago, when some fisheries biologists—without an okay from the bureaucracy, according to legend—backpacked fertile salmon eggs to the upper watershed and planted them. When the eggs hatched, the little fish, without fanfare, found their way downstream to the sea, only to return three years later as 20-pound adult king salmon fighting upstream to spawn. Volunteers carried the big fish over the falls that first year. The Tumwater fish ladders were subsequently constructed over the falls, and salmon have been returning annually ever since. It's a great show in late summer and fall.

�֍ Northwest Trek

State Highway 161, six miles north of Eatonville. 832-6117 or (800) 433-TREK. Daily, 9:30–dusk, March through October; Fridays and weekends, winter. Adults $7.50; children (5–17) $4; tots (3–4) $3.

The Trek is a unique and wonderful place to see native Northwest animals and birds living in 635 acres of almost-perfect natural surroundings. The philosophy here is that many children have seen tigers and lions and exotic animals from other parts of the globe, but they haven't seen the wild animals that live in their own backyards. This list includes black-tailed deer, elk, moose, beaver, woodland caribou, mountain goat, grizzly bear, bison, and wolves—animals so proud and beautiful they almost break your heart.

You ride a tram through the sanctuary, spotting animals as you go with the help of well-informed and entertaining naturalist guides. There are also a few special wildlife exhibits, including the opportunity to see bald and golden eagles close up.

Complete with picnic areas and food services, this is a great place for children's parties. Group rates are available upon request.

�֍ Tokul Creek Fish Hatchery

On Highway 202 between Fall City and Snoqualmie. 222-5464. Daily, 8–4:30. Free.

This is a trout and steelhead hatchery where little fish in various stages of development can be seen year round. There is an attractive picnic area adjacent to the hatchery.

✴ Issaquah Fish Hatchery
125 W. Sunset Way, Issaquah. 392-3180. Daily, 8–4:30. Free.

Another Washington State hatchery where some investment has been made in attractive and informative visitor facilities. Big adult king (Chinook) salmon predictably return to spawn in September and October. There are no tours, but excellent signage describes and explains what goes on here.

✴ Washington State Salmon Hatcheries
902-2250 (Olympia). Daily, 8–dusk. Free.

There are many Washington State salmon hatcheries. Recommended for Chinook salmon watching in September and October: Green River Hatchery on Black Diamond–Auburn Road outside Auburn; Samish Hatchery just outside Mount Vernon; Puyallup Hatchery outside Orting.

✴ Blue Heron Marsh
Federal Way Exit 143 from Interstate 5. Take 320th Street east (becomes Peasley Canyon Road) three miles to West Valley Highway. Turn right and immediately right again into parking lot. Free.

The major attractions here are great blue herons and their platform nests high atop the red alder trees. This former highway construction gravel pit was set aside for the birds who adopted it a few years ago, and there is a half-mile loop trail that provides excellent bird watching and some interpretation. Binoculars here are a must to get the most out of the bird watching, although you'll almost always see the herons—hard to miss them at four feet tall. You'll likely see the young herons in their nests in late spring to early summer. The juvenile birds are more brownish than their blue-gray parents but almost as big!

The stick nests, as large as four feet across, are numerous in the marsh. Sometimes there are several in a single tree.

✴ Wolf Haven America
311 Offut Lake Road (just off old Highway 99, 15 minutes south of Olympia), Tenino. 264-HOWL. Daily, 10–5, summer. Call for winter times, which vary. Adults $3.50; youths, $2.50; children under 5 free.

This is a cause as much as a destination, a very worthy cause. The 65-acre preserve is the home of some three dozen captive wolves displayed in large enclosures, but the Wolf Haven staff is principally dedicated to educating the public and school children about these magnificent, endangered animals. They regularly visit schools with wolves in tow, and on

Friday evenings through summer (7:30 to 10) they host "Howl-Ins" at Wolf Haven—songs, stories, and marshmallows around the campfire, and a chance to howl with the wolves.

Children certainly enjoy seeing the wolves, but in a time when both the U.S. Federal and Canadian Governments are still waging "war" on these lovely, rare creatures in the wild, the message at Wolf Haven seems to overshadow the novelty. As you read this, wolf populations in northern British Columbia are being controlled by a provincial government policy to "protect game animals," which makes little or no scientific sense but underscores why politics and science don't mix well.

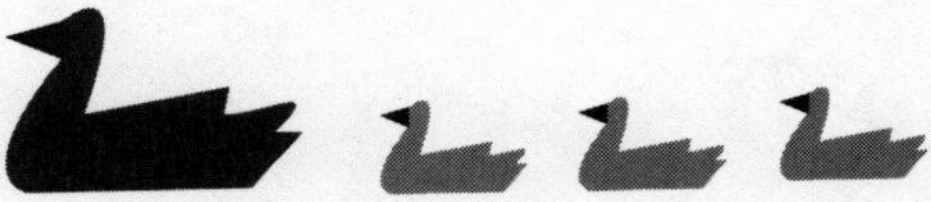

2
Tide Pools and Shorelines

Puget Sound is the Far West's largest inland sea, a complex of marine passages and fjords with a shoreline so rich in natural history it would take a lifetime to explore. Many beaches are easily accessible thanks to abundant parks and designated clamming and oyster-gathering areas administered by the Washington Department of Fisheries.

The discoveries you make will vary with the type of shoreline you explore. There are gravel beaches, mud beaches, salt marshes, beds of eelgrass, rocky bluffs, and long spits of sand. What they all have in common is a steep tide—as much as 15 vertical feet of it—that rises and falls twice each day. Within this intertidal zone lives a host of plants and animals whose lifestyles are both marine and terrestrial.

Many tideland explorers concentrate on the edible shorelife (see Chapter 4), but to most children the inedible critters are even more intriguing: "What is a goose barnacle, a chiton, an anemone?" Followed by "What does it do? What does it eat? Will it bite me?"

To biologists the intertidal zone is really several zones. There are creatures that tolerate only brief exposure to air and thus dwell near the low tide mark—sea urchins, for example. Others, such as acorn barnacles, require less water and live higher up in the "splash zone." Some, like California mussels, thrive in battering surf, while others, like clams, conceal themselves underground or in crevices so they won't be swept away. Some crabs move up and down the beach with impunity.

Terrain and wave action are your clues to which creatures live where. Boulders and rocks are homes for limpets, chitons, and snails. Permanently settled anemones and small darting sculpin reside in tidal pools on rocky shores.

A local tide table is an absolute necessity for exploring the intertidal zone. Averaging $1, they are widely available from general stores, boating/fishing supply outlets, and marinas throughout Western Washington. Throughout Puget Sound there are normally two complete tidal cycles, approximately every 24 hours. High and low tides thus run about six hours apart.

Basically, tides are created by the gravitational pull of the moon and sun and because the moon and sun behave predictably, the tides are predictable. There are other factors, however, and the tides do not always exactly match forecasts. For example, barometric pressure and winds may amplify or depress a tide. Shape, size, and bottom characteristics of a tidal basin greatly influence the range of tidal activity, which is why Puget Sound tides, ranging to·15 feet, are greater than those on the Washington Coast, where they average 12 feet.

On broad, gently sloping beaches even a modest rise or fall will cover or expose a great expanse of beach. It's wise to keep an eye on rising waters; on certain beaches an incoming tide may strand you on an island. Be cautious, too, about beaching a boat during an outgoing tide. It may leave you high and dry for as long as 12 hours. By consulting your tide table you can prevent these kinds of misadventures.

Beachcombing is not permitted on the shores of most Washington State parks; this applies to large pieces of driftwood, boulders, and the like. It's okay, however, to pick up shells and small rocks. Collecting live tide-pool creatures is never a good idea and is usually illegal, but they are wonderful to look at and photograph.

✳ Salt Creek Park
Eleven miles from U.S. Highway 101 (turn off four miles west of Port Angeles). 928-3441. 6–dusk. Free.

This 196-acre county park contains some of the best tide pools on the inland waters. It has a rocky shoreline rich with small tide-pool critters, including a large hermit crab population. These entertaining little guys borrow empty seashells for temporary housing, an interesting lesson in alternative lifestyles for young natural historians.

There are some old bunkers from World War II shore batteries in the park, which create surprisingly interesting backdrops for picnics. With the help of a little youthful imagination one can still sight cannons on ships in the Strait of Juan de Fuca...but don't pull the trigger!

✳ Dungeness Spit
(See Chapter 1, Dungeness National Wildlife Refuge)

Jutting seven-and-one-half miles into the windy Strait of Juan de Fuca, this remarkable piece of geography features, in addition to its splendid bird watching and clamming, a natural trap for flotsam on the west, or windward, side—driftwood, escaped fishing-net floats, hatch covers, seashells, even an occasional boat hull can be found here. Savvy beachcombers go out immediately after a good storm.

Just a few years ago it was customary to find Japanese glass fishing floats in such places, but today you're more likely to find plastic floats.

Clamming on Dungeness is on the eastern, leeward side of the spit.

Unlikely as it may seem, the area around Dungeness is in the "rain shadow" of the Olympic Mountains, with a rainfall of only 10 to 18 inches per year. One hundred fifty inches or more is the norm in the rain forests of the mountain range's Pacific slopes, just a few miles away.

✖ Fort Flagler State Park

On the northern end of Marrowstone Island (north of Port Ludlow). 385-1259. 6–dusk. Free.

Fort Flagler is big enough (780 acres) and far enough off main highways (you cross another island just to get there) to be a real adventure, and it contains several miles of beaches rich with driftwood, shells, flotsam, and other treasures. There's good crabbing and clamming. And there are some big-league bunkers and old cannons to organize for pint-sized military campaigns. Both inside and near Fort Flagler you'll see abundant wildflowers along the roads in May and June.

This is a wonderful park!

Flagler was one of three forts begun in 1897 that formed the "Triangle of Fire" or "Death Triangle." Fort Warden at Port Townsend and Fort Casey on Whidbey Island were the other points on the triangle, a defense against enemy ships misguided enough to enter Admiralty Inlet. Apparently word got out to the enemy and no sea invasions were launched. The fort was reactivated during World War II and turned over to Washington State in 1955.

A printed folder with a map of the park's roads and points of interest is available at headquarters.

✖ Deception Pass State Park

On the northern end of Whidbey Island and the southern end of Fidalgo Island (connected by a bridge). 675-2417. 6–dusk. Free.

This is a huge, 4,000-acre park with miles of shoreline, including some of the best rocky tide pools in the Puget Sound region. Rosario Beach on the Fidalgo Island side of the park is a favorite tide-pool study area for biology classes (no collecting!). It's a rich preserve with surprises and discoveries awaiting both amateur and professional marine biologists.

An awesome spectacle, to be seen during tidal changes, is the two-and-one-half billion gallons an hour of water that course through Deception Pass between the two islands. The average flow is six to seven knots, sometimes faster.

✳ Fort Casey State Park
Midway on the west side of Whidbey Island at Admiralty Point. 678-4519. 6–dusk. Free.

Fort Casey was one of the points on the hyperbolic "Death Triangle" (see Fort Flagler, earlier in this chapter). Those historic years are relived every time the kids are turned loose on the parapets and bunkers of the old fort.

Look for starfish and other tidal-zone life on the rocks of the jetty by the ferry dock. Admiralty Head is the Whidbey Island ferry terminal for the Port Townsend ferry crossing.

✳ Discovery Park
The northwest portion of Magnolia Bluff, Seattle. 386-4236. 6–dusk. Free.

If Seattle weren't blessed by so many magnificent parks, it might well become famous for Discovery Park, the former Fort Lawton, a U.S. Army legacy dating back to 1896. Ownership was transferred to Seattle in 1972.

For young beach explorers there is an excellent beach here, along with sand dunes, meadows, green forests, and some magnificent views of Puget Sound.

The Daybreak Star Arts Center, adjacent to the park, contains an excellent, representative collection of Indian and Alaskan Native art and hosts cultural programs through the year, including a popular salmon barbecue (285-4425).

✳ Saltwater State Park
Just off Marine View Drive (Highway 509) between Des Moines and Dash Point. 764-4128. 6–dusk. Free.

Just 88 acres with 1,445 feet of beach, this is another one of those Puget Sound parks that would be extraordinary if it were located any place but Puget Sound. It has an especially nice beach for toddlers. In summer, sunlight warms the water over a shallow sandy bottom on the park's tidelands, creating a choice wading place.

An artificial reef 150 yards offshore attracts marine life, which in turn attracts skin and scuba divers. There are picnic tables and a concession stand open summers.

✳ Dash Point State Park
Just southwest of Federal Way via S.W. Dash Point Road (Highway 509). 593-2206. 6–dusk. Free.

With a half-mile of choice wading beach and six miles of forested trails, this is another fine park for families. The beach is gently sloping, and the shallow tidelands are sun-warmed in summer. During minus tides as much as 2,000 feet of beach is exposed! There is much intertidal life here.

✵ Kopachuck State Park

Six miles from Gig Harbor over rural roads, well marked by signs. 265-3606. 6–dusk. Free.

A long sandy exposure at low tide makes this a good driftwood beach anytime. This is a good sand dollar environment, judging by the number found here. There is about a half-mile of shoreline at Kopachuck, with good beachcombing, some clam digging, warm water for summer wading, and Puget Sound viewscapes offshore. There are short, forested walking trails and picnic areas with sunlight filtered through firs and alders.

3

Big Game Hunting in the Tidelands

The name of the game is clams. Nimble children can catch crabs and oysters, too, around Puget Sound, but clamming is the almost sure-fire family sport—lots of fun, and the payoff is delicious. A culinary tip: Youngsters who show little enthusiasm for clam chowder will often warm to clam fritters.

The best clamming and crabbing tides are "minus tides," or tides that are lower than average. They expose more beach than usual. It's best to arrive an hour or two before predicted low tide. The same marinas and stores that provide tide tables also carry Washington State shellfishing regulations, which are generous but must be followed, including the rule of filling your digging holes, an important conservation practice.

The most common clams, and easiest to dig, are the bay clams, the catchall term for: Washington clam, quahog, beef steak *(Saxidomus giganteus)*, cockle, basket cockle *(Clinocarium nuttalli)*, native littleneck, rock clam, butter clam *(Protobacha staminea)*, Japanese littleneck, Manila clam *(Venerupis japonica)*, mud clam, eastern soft-shell clam *(Mya arenaria)*, and bentnose clam *(Macoma nasuta)*. Collectively, these all look like "clams."

The big game of Puget Sound clams is the geoduck *(Panope generosa)*, pronounced *gooey-duck,* an ungainly, bulging critter averaging 3 pounds and capable of growing to 20. It's highly prized for its flavor and is a challenge to excavate, requiring tides of minus two or lower and digs of three feet or more.

The other big clam is the gaper or horse clam *(Tresus capax)*, which is not prized for flavor but often finds its way into chowders.

For children, bay clams are the perfect big game, satisfying the basic instincts of hunting, fishing, farming, and making mud pies all in one gloriously simple operation.

And they don't bite!

Crabs do bite (pinch, actually), but where they are common they are sporty to catch. The male Dungeness crab *(Cancer magister)* is the choicest game. The smaller, similarly shaped red crab *(Cancer productus)* is also good to eat. It has red and black-lined pincers and knows how to use them. The best crabbing is in beds of eelgrass around Puget Sound. Crab hunting is not recommended for young children, but it's a great sport for older kids.

Where they occur, oysters are almost too easy to gather, but the law requires that they must be shucked (removed from their shells) on the beach, and this isn't much fun for youngsters...unless they acquire a taste for oysters. Then watch 'em shuck!

A word of caution about "Red Tides": The algae in water sometimes produces a condition commonly called Red Tide, which is associated with making shellfish toxic. The poison is produced by a colorless algae (*Gonyaulax cantenella*) which, when concentrated in shellfish that are eaten, causes paralytic poisoning. Only bivalves (clams, mussels, oysters) are a potential danger. Finfish, crabs, shrimp, and abalone are not affected. Washington State provides a toll-free "Red Tide Hotline" number to call for current beach closures: 1-800-562-5632. Always consult this number before gathering shellfish.

✹ Old Fort Townsend State Park

Turn off State Highway 113, four miles southwest of Port Townsend. 385-4730.

This 377-acre park features almost a mile of beach for low-tide clamming and crabbing. There are nature trails, picnic tables, and boat-moorages. A path to the beach begins on a bluff next to an interpretive display.

The old fort was built to protect Port Townsend during the Indian Wars of 1856–57, but by the time the fort was ready for service the wars were over.

✹ Shine Tidelands State Park

North of the west end of Hood Canal Floating Bridge via the first right turn, a dirt road, off Highway 104 past the bridge. Free for day use.

This bivalve-rich beach overlooks the entrance to Hood Canal, and in addition to clam digging you may see a nuclear submarine ghosting by now and then (if it's running on the surface). This can be a good place to find great big geoducks, and for that reason it is appropriate to blindfold anyone you bring to this park and swear them to secrecy. That's how we learned about it! And respect adjacent property boundaries: The local landowners are a little touchy.

Geoducks, the largest clam species in Washington, require some real effort to excavate, as well as very low tides, but the smaller bay clam species provide nice sport for children. Should mom and dad dig for ducks, they can certainly expect helpful hints and supervision from small fry.

✴ Seal Rock Forest Camp

U.S. Highway 101, two miles north of Brinnon. 765-3368. Free for day use.

A broad beach with a forested backdrop where the oyster gathering can be especially good during low tides.

✴ Dosewallips State Park

U.S. Highway 101, just north of Brinnon 796-4415. Dawn to dusk. Free.

This is another possible clamming and oyster-gathering beach that there's no need to tell the world about, and in fact its shellfishing prospects have been dicey. It was over harvested in years past, made a heroic comeback, and most recently has been contaminated by a resident seal population. Rangers have built a fence to keep the seals off the oyster beaches, but the results were not known at press time. The Dosewallips River, which roars playfully as it races out of the Olympic Mountains, fans across the park's beach into Hood Canal and creates near-perfect conditions for growing bivalves. The river also creates minor logistical problems for walking across the beach: Plan on wet feet here. The campground is a great place for kids to ride their bikes and for families to take short day hikes.

✴ Department of Natural Resources Beaches

Boat access only, on both the Dabob Bay and Hood Canal sides of the Toandos Peninsula. Free.

Most Department of Natural Resources boat-access-only beaches are "underutilized," a euphemism that indicates the presence of good shellfishing. Department of Natural Resources Beaches 57 and 57B are boat access only and are marked on boating recreation charts. Most of these beaches are publicly owned only to the high tide mark, so you must come and go by water, and you may not camp on the beaches.

Small boats are available for rent on Hood Canal (see Chapter 5), and there are boat-launching ramps on Quilcene Bay, at Whitney Point on Dabob Bay, and at Seabeck on the east side of Hood Canal.

✴ Potlatch State Park

On U.S. Highway 101, just south of Potlatch on Hood Canal. Dawn to dusk. Free.

Hood Canal is a seafood resource epitomized by Potlatch State Park at the waterway's southern end. Here you'll find clams, and a host of other good things to eat. The area attracts crowds, but the mood is always congenial.

In summer the Hood Canal waters reach 70 degrees; tempting for swimming. As a rule, swimming access is better at any of several private resorts than in the public parks. Don't dive deep, however, or you'll pass through the thermocline where the warm top layer of water meets the bone-chilling lower layer of cold water. The warm water is usually about 10 feet deep around mid-July. The cold water is about 600 feet deep. Hood Canal, carved by glaciers, seems bottomless.

Belfair State Park

Almost at the very end of Hood Canal via State Highway 300 from Belfair. 478-4625. Dawn to dusk. Free.

An excellent swimming area and large playground make this a wonderful park for children. Oyster hunting is good at low tide, and the park and surrounding forests are world-famous for wild rhododendrons, which usually bloom in May.

Scenic Beach State Park

On the east side of Hood Canal at Seabeck. Dawn to dusk. Free.

Oysters have made a strong comeback here recently (after a closed-to-oyster-gathering period). There is a play area for children. From Misery Point near the park, it's a short boat trip across the canal to Fisherman Harbor State Park Recreation Tideland (at the southern end of Toandos Peninsula), where oyster hunting is excellent.

Camano Island State Park

On the west side of Camano Island at the end of West Camano Drive. 387-3031. Dawn to dusk. Free.

This is a lovely park, far enough from traffic to assure light visitor use most of the time. Clamming for "steamers" is excellent over a mile-long stretch of beach, from which you can watch boat traffic on Saratoga Passage.

There are three miles of forested walking trails including a half-mile, self-guided nature walk.

Penrose Point State Park

South of Lakebay (about three miles from Longbranch) via Shelgren Lorentz Road and Bayview Avenue. 884-2514. Dawn to dusk. Free.

This 135-acre park contains almost two miles of shoreline with some good clam digging. Forested highlands provide hiking paths and picnic areas.

The best clam digging is on the half-mile-long sand spit in Mayo Cove that is exposed during minus tides.

✳ Puget Sound Public Shellfish Sites (Information)

State of Washington, Department of Fisheries, P.O. Box 43135, Olympia, Washington 98504-3136. 902-2200.

The Department of Natural Resources administers dozens of beaches around Puget Sound where you can find outstanding clam digging and oyster gathering. Many of these beaches can only be reached by boat, the appropriate way to gain access without crossing private property. Others can be reached by car. Write or call the Department of Fisheries for maps showing the locations of these beaches. There are bonanzas among these beaches for the family in search of shellfish!

4
Fishing Piers

Pier fishing has a lot to recommend it for children and parents, too. It is especially good around Puget Sound, both in the Sound and in nearby freshwater lakes. Unlike boats, piers allow escape from boredom. Tired of fishing? Get up, stretch, walk around, and explore the area.

A very young child, or any child unable to swim, should wear a life preserver on a pier. It provides both safety for children and peace of mind for mom and dad.

Some of the best choices among piers are the several public fishing docks around Lake Washington. Fishery experts point out that Lake Washington is underutilized by fishermen. It is rich in both resident and migratory fish—trout, crappie, bass, kokanee (land-locked salmon), steelhead (migratory rainbow trout), and migrating salmon and catfish.

Try this basic Lake Washington hookup from the piers: Line to a one- or two-ounce sinker; 18-inch two- to four-pound test leader from sinker to size six or eight hook; bait hook with two or three salmon eggs and a marshmallow *or* a worm and a marshmallow. Fish this rig from the end of the pier on the bottom, keeping the line taut from the rod to the sinker so you can "feel" the bottom. The marshmallow floats the eggs or worm just off the bottom where, with patience and luck, a passing trout will bite. There are many ways to catch fish in Lake Washington: This one practically comes with a guarantee.

It's a good idea to use a small landing net when fishing from piers, as many fish are lost when "lifted" out of the water on the line.

For the adventurous, consider night fishing for squid. Squid, or *calamari* in Italian, migrate into the Strait of Juan de Fuca and down Puget Sound in the fall. They move farther south and grow larger in size as the season progresses, reaching a foot in length by December. Squid are attracted to strong light over water. Incandescent lamps (white light) and sodium-vapor lamps (orange) are the best attractors. Bluish mercury-vapor lamps aren't enticing. Pick a dark night when your lamplight won't compete with moonlight. Try to fish on high, slack tides when it is not raining.

Most squid fishermen use lightweight rods and reels with about four-pound test line rigged with up to four "squid jigs." Place a one- or two-ounce sinker at the end of the line. And dress warmly: Cold nights are usually best for catching squid.

Some pier fishermen bring a crab pot along to try their luck at trapping a legal crab while they fish. An even surer bet on some freshwater piers is crayfish trapping. Crab and crayfish traps are available in most fishing tackle stores. Along with fishing, tending a dockside crab or crayfish trap provides another activity for peripatetic youngsters.

Just about every fishing pier has an "old guy." An "old guy" can be 18 to 80. What qualifies him as an "old guy" is that he fishes from the pier all the time and he's a fountain of wisdom on how to fish it. He knows types of tackle and lures, and the best tides, wind directions, temperatures, and times of day to fish. Always talk to the "old guy" when you find him.

Sporting goods stores carry current fishing regulations, which in Washington are regrettably complicated and laborious to decipher. They are described in the free 40-page annual publication *Washington Game Fish Seasons and Regulations.* If you can't obtain a copy in your tackle shop, write Washington Department of Game, 600 N. Capitol Way, Olympia, WA 98504. Despite their complicated written regulations, the Department of Game personnel are always friendly and helpful to talk with.

✳ Edmonds Public Fishing Pier
At the foot of Dayton Street, Edmonds. Saltwater. Free.

Mostly bottom fish here, but there's always the possibility that a migrating salmon will take your lure. This is a good squid fishing pier in winter. There's also plenty of boating activity, including regular comings and goings of the Edmonds–Kingston Washington State ferries.

✳ Pier 57, Seattle
On Seattle's waterfront at the foot of University Street. Saltwater. Free.

Part of Seattle's revitalized waterfront, Pier 57 has a big observation deck with good views of Elliott Bay and its harbor traffic. There are fishing holes in the heavy-timbered deck, complete with small benches. Folks catch bottom fish here, a salmon now and then, and squid in the winter. The Seattle Aquarium (Chapter 1) is nearby, along with several restaurants and stands to purchase a crab cocktail or fish and chips.

✳ Des Moines Public Fishing Pier
At the foot of S. 227th Street, Des Moines. Saltwater. Free.

This 670-foot pier provides some excellent pier fishing thanks to an adjacent artificial reef. The "old guys" claim you can catch just about any fish that dwells in Puget Sound here. The bottom fishing is very good, and this is another recommended squidding pier. There are a half-dozen nearby restaurants and seafood bars.

✳ Les Davis Pier, Tacoma

Off Rustin Way, one mile northwest of McCarver Street. Saltwater. Free.

Also called the "Old Town Dock," this fishing pier is adjacent to an artificial reef that lures bottom fish, cod, squid, and sometimes salmon. There are covered tables and picnic areas at the far side of the pier, all part of recently refurbished Commencement Park. The park also contains sand boxes for toddlers and some pretty good beachcombing.

✳ Harper City Park

At Harper, 1.5 miles from the Southworth Ferry Terminal (Fauntleroy Ferry). Saltwater. Free.

The venerable wharf here is now a city park with a long fishing pier. Marine life on the old pier's pilings attracts fish, and the shallow (30-foot) bottom makes the logistics of pier fishing easy. This is a good crabbing spot at times. The Fauntleroy Ferry trip to Southworth, with an intermediate stop at Vashon Island, is a nice day's outing from West Seattle.

✳ Capitol Lake, Olympia

Parallel to the railroad tracks, Capitol Lake Park in Olympia. Freshwater. Dawn to dusk. Free.

This attractive pier on the capitol city's 300-acre lake is a popular lunch spot for state government office workers and an excellent spot to catch trout and, during open season, salmon. When the fish are biting there are usually a lot of "old guys" here.

✳ Pine Lake

Four miles north of Issaquah via 226th Avenue N.E. Dawn to dusk. Free.

There is a county park on the east shore with a public fishing pier. The 86-acre lake is planted each year with both fry- and legal-size rainbow trout. As a rule, the fishing improves from the summer to fall. There are a few bass here, too.

✳ Logboom Park, Lake Washington

From Bothell Way, turn south on 61st Avenue N.E. Dawn to dusk. Restrooms. Free.

This King County park contains a long L-shaped pier at the south end of the parking lot. The water is shallow, even at the end of the pier,

but it is located near the point where the Sammamish River flows into
Lake Washington, and folks have been known to catch some big fish here.

✸ Waverly Park, Lake Washington
North on Waverly Way from Market Street in Kirkland. Dawn to dusk.
Restrooms (closed in winter). Free.

   This small finger pier is a good trout fishing prospect in fall and
winter. Try bottom fishing with salmon eggs.

✸ Marina Park, Lake Washington
Downtown Kirkland (at the foot of Central Way N.E.). Dawn to dusk.
Restrooms. Free.

   This is a large public boat dock adjacent to downtown Kirkland, with
many nearby shops and restaurants, an attractive city park, and ducks to
feed. It's another good trout fishing spot in fall and winter.

✸ Enatai Beach Park, Lake Washington
Underneath the Interstate 90 Bridge in Bellevue. Take the Bellevue Way exit
from Interstate 90 and turn left on 113th Avenue N.E. (which becomes S.E.
34th Street). Dawn to dusk. Restrooms. Free.

   There are two piers in this Bellevue city park. The best fishing is
from the smaller pier to the north, directly under the freeway bridge. It's a
little crowded here sometimes, mostly with fellows who seem to fish the
pier regularly. Perhaps they know something!

✸ Gene Coulon Memorial Beach Park, Lake Washington
In Renton, exit Park Avenue N. from Interstate 405 and turn right onto Lake
Washington Boulevard. Dawn to dusk. Restrooms. Free.

   This large Renton park is the newest major park development on
Lake Washington, with many docks and piers available to fishermen. It's
located near the mouth of the Cedar River, a fish migration route.

✸ Seward Park, Lake Washington
The park entrance is on Lake Washington Boulevard in Seattle, near the foot
of Orcas Street. Dawn to dusk. Restrooms. Free.

   This lovely, large Seattle city park is on a peninsula in Lake Washington and provides a wealth of good bank fishing. But most fishermen hover
around the entrance to the University of Washington fish hatchery on the
south shore, near the park's tennis court parking lot. There is also a fishing pier near the northwestern tip of the park.

Seward Park's flowering cherry trees and rhododendron plantings are spectacular in spring.

✻ Washington Park Arboretum/Waterfront Trail, Seattle

On University of Washington Campus, Seattle (see Chapter 5).

This extraordinary system of parks, waterside paths, and nature trails provides some excellent fishing along with many other attractions: wildlife watching, people watching, spring blossoms, fall colors, and year-round cheer. Good prospects for fishing are from the piers and waterfront trails on the eastern portions of Lake Union, the Foster Island Trail, and the Union Bay Waterfront Trail (most easily accessible from the Museum of History and Industry parking lot).

Crayfish are common in many places, including this portion of the Lake Washington waterways. What to use to bait crayfish traps is endlessly discussed, but in truth the delicious crustaceans are not particular. Bacon scraps are time honored. Believe it or not, corn on the cob is a dynamite crayfish bait. Some of the most productive crayfish trappers around swear by it and bring home buckets of crayfish to prove it.

The marshes on and around Foster Island are a rich wildlife habitat. In addition to trout, there are bass, crappie, and freshwater perch here.

5

Boating

As you study a map of the Puget Sound region you'll notice a lot of water. And if you happen to overlook this fact, the child in your family will not.

It's claimed there are more boats per capita around Puget Sound than anywhere else in the world, yet except for a few key waterways (the Lake Washington Ship Canal, for example) there is so much water that you can always find some solitude afloat.

Most of Puget Sound, as well as the hundreds of freshwater lakes that decorate the region's forests, were carved by glaciers or left in the wake of retreating glaciers as the last great ice age melted away. The fjords of Puget Sound are incredibly deep—over 600 feet in places—yet because of the phenomena of thermoclines, some of the waterways are warm enough for surface swimming during the summer. Narrow Hood Canal is especially nice for summer swimming and boating, with plenty of public boat launching facilities (see pages 18–20).

A jewel among the lakes is 22-mile long Lake Washington, separating Seattle from the "eastside communities" of Bellevue and Kirkland. It isn't fair to say residents of Seattle take Lake Washington for granted, but it's a testimonial to how much recreational water there is in Western Washington that Lake Washington isn't more widely lionized as one of the urban wonders of the world!

From canoes to ocean-going freighters, a remarkable range of boat rentals is available in Western Washington. For a day's outing with children, only small boats on calm waters are described here.

All boat-rental operations provide life preservers, and small children should always use them. Better still, especially for very small kids, purchase a life preserver that is fitted to the child. The "child-size" preservers provided with rental boats often don't fit well. Seat-cushion (buoyant cushion, Type IV) preservers are not much good for anyone's safety, and they are absolutely worthless for the boating safety of a child.

As a general rule of boating, everyone has a better time when the entire crew are comfortable swimmers.

The hours listed for boat rental firms apply during the summer season. Call for winter season hours, which often fluctuate with changes in weather conditions.

�֎ Center for Wooden Boats

1010 Valley Street, Seattle (south side of Lake Union). 382-2628. Wednesday through Monday, 12–6. Rentals, $6 to $15 per hour.

The Center is a small-craft museum where you can rent classically constructed wooden rowboats and sailboats, gems of workmanship that often provide fond memories for older parents and grandparents. There is some small-boat traffic at this end of Lake Union, but strict seven-knot speed limits are well-enforced. This is an "urban" boating experience, with plenty of lively maritime activity against the high-rise backdrop of nearby downtown Seattle. You'll almost certainly see the comings and goings of float planes at this end of Lake Union.

The Center sponsors several special events each year, including the Wooden Boat Show on the Fourth-of-July weekend, and field trips for children which include sailing a circa 1900 30-foot fishing boat.

✖ Sailboat Rentals and Charters

2046 Westlake N., Seattle. 281-9176. Rentals, $15 to $25 per hour; $85 to $165 per day.

A day of sailing on Lake Washington or Puget Sound is a wonderful family activity if you have an experienced sailor among you. It may seem expensive, but it's probably a bargain compared to owning and maintaining your own sailboat. Available boats range from 14 to 30 feet, and a couple of families might share a day on a larger boat. Overnight charters and sailing lessons are available.

This company also charters sailboats out of Anacortes, gateway to the San Juan Islands.

✖ Northwest Outdoor Boat Center

1009 N.E. Boat Street, Seattle (on Portage Bay). 632-1984. Weekdays, 10–6; weekends, 10–8. Kayaks, $6 and up per hour; $16 and up all day.

These remarkable boats are capturing the attention of many small boaters. The double kayaks are best for younger children. Single kayaks are more fun for older kids. You can use the kayaks locally, or you can arrange to "cartop" them off for a day or a weekend. The center will provide you with a roof rack if you don't have your own.

✖ University of Washington Waterfront Activity Center

Southeast of Husky Stadium, via Montlake Boulevard, Seattle. 543-9433. Daily, 10–dusk. Canoes, $3 per hour. Arrive early on sunny summer days.

This is possibly the best boating bargain in the Northwest. From the canoe dock, you can dart across the Montlake Cut waterway into the tules, cattails, and water lilies around Foster Island and the Arboretum. You canoe right under the freeway, and there's always a world of activity, including geese and ducks, lazy-day students, passing yachts, drifting fishermen, and turtles basking on half-submerged logs. This really is a floating "garden" through the long summer months, and a pleasure to explore just about anytime.

Anglers catch bass here among the water lilies, and there are crappie and freshwater perch. Seldom seen during daylight hours is a large muskrat population. And many kinds of birds call the marsh home.

✷ Enatai Beach Park

On Lake Washington in Bellevue, just south of Interstate 909 (see Chapter 4). 453-1729. Wednesday through Friday, 4–8; weekends, 10–6. Canoes, $2.50 per hour; kayaks, $6 and up.

Boating traffic in the channel between Bellevue and Mercer Islands is usually well-mannered, and it's fun to poke along the shoreline to view the waterfront houses and docks. If you've thought about doing some kayak camping—an activity growing in popularity on Puget Sound— this is a good, safe place for the family to practice handling the attractive, sleek boats.

Canoes are a little "tipsy," and young children should always be encouraged to kneel or sit on the *bottom* of the canoe (not on the "seats") to keep the center of gravity low. If the wake of passing boats heads your way, turn the bow of the canoe into the wake. Head on, canoes will take remarkably rough water.

✷ Gene Coulon Memorial Beach Park

1201 Lake Washington Boulevard N., Renton (at the very southeast end of Lake Washington). 235-2568. Daily, 10–8. Rowboats, paddleboats, canoes, sailboards, $6 to $10 per hour.

Here's a vast fleet of rental boats to choose from, with nice small-boat sailing water and without a lot of fast boat traffic.

✷ Greenlake Boat Rentals

7351 E. Greenlake Drive N., Seattle. 527-0171. May 31 through September 10, daily, about 10–7. Paddleboats, canoes, rowboats, sailboats, $6 to $12 per hour.

This is Seattle's "other lake," an attractive park well known for its jogging path and its "super ducks." It is a perfect small-boating place for young children, with no motor boats allowed.

The "super ducks" are a large, hybrid cross between wild and domestic mallard ducks and are reported to chase large dogs, scare horses, and intimidate burly police patrolmen! They never attack canoes, however, and they provide an interesting topic of conversation as you drift across the gentle waters of Greenlake.

✸ Seacrest Boat House

1660 Harbor Avenue S.W. (on Elliott Bay, West Seattle). 932-1050. Wednesday through Sunday, dawn to dusk. Boat with motor, $10 per hour; rowboat, $10 per day.

This is a good place to take an older youngster salmon fishing. The waters of Elliott Bay are usually calm, the fishing is remarkably good when the salmon are running, and there are no long distances to travel over water. As a bonus, there are often a few exotic, foreign freighters at anchor.

✸ Point Defiance Boathouse

Point Defiance Park, Tacoma. 591-5325. Dawn to dusk. 14-foot "kicker" boats, $12 per day without motor, $44 per day with motor and gas.

This is another good choice for taking youngsters salmon fishing on waters that are predictably calm most of the time. You can bring a salmon to net just yards from shore here. The venerable boathouse burned to the ground and was rebuilt in 1988, so the tradition and nostalgia continue into the next generation. The "new" boathouse also contains marine supplies, fishing tackle, and a restaurant.

✸ Sport Fishing of Seattle

Seattle Harbor Tours, Pier 55, Seattle. 623-1445. Adults $62; children $42, for 6-to-7 hour charter fishing trips.

For the older child, an all-day sport fishing charter can be quite an adventure and very comfortable on the sheltered, inland waters of Puget Sound. Tackle is provided. Salmon, of course, are the game fish in the Sound, but there are many other equally delicious species of cod and rock fish to be caught from the inland waters. Sport Fishing of Seattle guarantees that each customer will catch at least one edible fish or their next boarding pass will be free. Even on warm summer days it's a wise precaution to carry an extra layer of clothing, as well as rain gear. Marine weather can change very quickly.

6

Ride a Ferry

Simply stated, the Washington State Marine Highway system and its ferryboats represent the best cruise bargains in the world. The ferries provide commuters with daily transportation across Puget Sound; they provide travelers to the region with access to some of the choicest getaways in Western Washington; and they provide wonderful day outings for everyone. For a few dollars you can cruise over inland waters and through misty, forested archipelagos. You can stand on the bow with the wind in your face, or retreat to the boat's roomy, heated public rooms to watch the scenery through big picture windows. You can comfortably lunch aboard, in the ferryboat coffee shop, or pack your own picnic. And for convenience, you can bring your car along. But you don't have to. Pedestrians (with or without bicycles) are welcome on the Puget Sound ferries.

Washington State Ferries issue current ferry schedules, which are available free at all ferry terminals and by mail. Savvy Puget Sound travelers keep a current schedule handy in their cars. Write Washington State Ferries, Colman Dock, Seattle, WA 98104. The statewide toll-free number is: 1-800-84-FERRY. In Seattle, call 464-6400.

✯ Seattle–Bremerton

From Pier 52, at the foot of Marion Street, to Bremerton. Crossing: 60 minutes.

Bremerton, home of a large U.S. naval shipyard, is also gateway to the Kitsap Peninsula—almost a small continent in itself. Geologically it just missed becoming an island. Had the glaciers that carved the north side of Case Inlet progressed another two miles to meet the glaciers of Lynch Cove on Hood Canal, Kitsap would have been the largest island in the conterminous United States.

In Bremerton you can visit the small Puget Sound Naval Shipyard Museum in the ferry terminal (open Wednesday through Sunday, from 10 to 4).

On Highway 3 along Sinclair Inlet, about two-and-a-half miles from the ferry terminal, the Navy routinely keeps one or two mothballed ships at dock for the public to visit. The USS *Missouri* was moored here for several years, but was returned to service in 1984. She is missed by kids

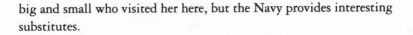

big and small who visited her here, but the Navy provides interesting substitutes.

⚝ Seattle–Winslow

From Pier 52, at the foot of Marion Street, to Winslow. Crossing: 35 minutes.

On any list of the "ten best places to live in the United States," you will almost always find Bainbridge Island. Most of its residents commute to Seattle. Three parks are choice candidates for a picnic and family outing.

Fay-Bainbridge State Park is 17 acres of wooded hillside with nature trails, boat launching, day-use kitchens, and play areas with horseshoe pits. The park also has a bathhouse with showers. Picnic areas, play fields, two tennis courts, and a jogging track with fitness stations accommodate the visitor to 90-acre Battle Point Park. And there's a small pond, usually well populated with ducks. Fort Ward State Park spreads out over 480 acres; its major attraction is a one-mile long beach popular with swimmers and scuba divers. The park also offers wooded trails, boat launching, and picnic areas. And there are some spectacular views of Puget Sound and its boating traffic.

⚝ Fauntleroy–Vashon Island–Southworth

Fauntleroy Ferry dock, West Seattle, at the foot of Fauntleroy Avenue, to Vashon Island. Crossing: 15 minutes. Vashon to Southworth on the Kitsap Peninsula. Crossing: 10 minutes.

Vashon Island and its smaller appendage, Maury Island, are a pleasure to explore. Or, if you are touring, in less than an hour you can travel from West Seattle to Southworth via two ferry voyages. On Vashon-Maury, stop in the sleepy little town of Vashon, where you'll find a bunch of touristy shops that are genuinely fun. There are cafes, a serious restaurant or two, a pastry shop, a natural food store, and a bakery. Nearby, Beall Greenhouses (17 of them) is world famous for its orchids, and Books by the Way, a renovated old feedstore, deserves a visit. Three county parks are located on Vashon-Maury:

Point Robinson Park, on the eastern-most point on Maury Island, has day-use picnic areas overlooking Point Robinson Lighthouse. Driftwood covers miles of beaches in both directions from the lighthouse.

Dockton Park is a quiet place well suited to small children. It contains playground equipment, a kitchen shelter, picnic tables with stoves, and a big lawn to run on. There is a boat launching and a long pier used by swimmers in summer.

Burton Acres Park (Jensen Point) occupies its own little peninsula. It has a small beach area, boat launching, and some picnic tables, but its great appeal is a bit of just-shy-of rain forest. Short trails take you through mossy old forest growth, past massive nurse stumps with ferns and huckleberry growing from them, and over carpets of vanilla leaf and club moss—an enchanted forest for imaginative youngsters.

✳ Edmonds–Kingston

From downtown Edmonds to Kingston, on the North Kitsap Peninsula. Crossing: 30 minutes.

Kingston has a crafts shop or two, and there are nice views from The Kingston Inn restaurant at the ferry terminal. There are also picnic tables with marine views on a spot of lawn at the Kingston Cove Marina.

It's a short drive to Point No Point. The lighthouse, built in 1897, is open for tours from 10 to noon and 1 to 3, Wednesday through Sunday. The driftwood-strewn Point No Point Beach is a national historic site, the location of the 1855 treaty that transferred most of Puget Sound from Indian ownership to the United States Government.

✳ Mukilteo–Clinton

From downtown Mukilteo to Clinton (Columbia Beach) on Whidbey Island. Crossing: 20 minutes.

Whidbey Island is the quintessence of rural Puget Sound, a large island of small farms and forests, secluded beaches, and tiny hamlets originally settled by retired sea captains. It has wonderful parks to explore: Deception Pass, Fort Casey (discussed in Chapter 2), and South Whidbey; historic Coupeville (see Chapter 8); and miles of quiet roads for meandering by car or bicycle.

South Whidbey State Park contains some exceptional forests and a sandy beach popular for swimming and agate hunting. Across the road from the park's entrance is a 225-acre tract of virgin forest, one of the last original stands of Douglas fir in the state. Its fate is uncertain.

One could spend weeks exploring Whidbey Island. A friend who grew up there likes to say how glad he was to leave such a sleepy, dull place. Having said that, he then proceeds to reminisce by the hour about his salubrious childhood.

✳ Anacortes–San Juan Islands–Sidney, B.C.

Via the islands of Lopez, Shaw, Orcas, and San Juan. Crossing: about 3.5 hours. You can get off at any of the islands. To avoid long waits during summer, leave your car in Anacortes and walk aboard.

This is the most scenic boat trip in the Pacific Northwest for any price. It takes you out of Puget Sound all the way to Vancouver Island, British Columbia, or you can tarry on any of the four picture-perfect San

Juan Islands served by ferries. There are about 200 islands in all. The San Juan Islands are deservedly popular with bicyclists, who come by ferry to tour for just a day or for weeks.

Orcas Island is a beautiful retreat with several resorts, including the landmark Rosario Resort, as well as many others with rustic beach cottages. Five-thousand-acre Moran State Park provides campsites, picnic tables, hot showers and other comforts, miles of hiking trails, lake swimming, boat rentals, and trout fishing. All that and not a single saltwater beach! Mount Constitution, 2,400 feet high, provides a superb 360-degree view of all of the San Juan Islands.

One of San Juan Island's most interesting attractions for children is San Juan National Historic Park, which commemorates the almost famous Pig War of 1859. In this border dispute between the British and Americans the only casualty was a British-owned pig shot by an American. No less than Kaiser Wilhelm of Germany mediated, finally placing San Juan Island on the American side of the future United States–Canadian boundary.

Whale watching from San Juan Island's far side is another rare attraction. And there is a Whale Watching Museum at Friday Harbor, three blocks from the ferry terminal. Fall is the time to watch the whales during their annual migrations.

Lopez Island and even sleepier Shaw Island have very limited camping, but they are wonderful places to escape to. Lopez has a pretty road system, well suited to bicycling. The road shoulders are narrow, but the island's residents drive courteously. There are some small restaurants and general stores on Lopez.

If you take the ferry all the way to Sidney, B.C., and on to Victoria, take the kids to the Provincial Museum. It's the world's great repository of Coastal Indian culture and the natural history of Canada, all beautifully interpreted and displayed.

7

Museums, Exhibits, and Visible History

Western Washington has its rich share of museums, science centers, special exhibits, and visible history. Seattle alone offers an amazing number of rainy day places to visit—whether it's raining or not. The only caveat is to be sure the museums selected are of real interest to children. Few art museums and galleries are included here because although many of us feel small children should be exposed to art appreciation early in life, children don't seem to agree. Hanging art bores most small kids. The fact that you can't climb on display cases seems to have something to do with this. It's safe to say that the more "hands-on" orientation an attraction has, the more it will appeal to young children.

✻ Whatcom Museum of History and Art/Children's Museum Northwest

121 Prospect Street, Bellingham. 676-6981. Tuesday through Sunday, noon– 5. Adults $2; children (under 12) $1. The adjacent Children's Museum is open Thursday through Saturday, 10–5. Adults and children $2; includes admission to Whatcom Museum.

Overlooking Bellingham Bay, the historic, three-story museum and gallery contains dioramas and photographs depicting scenes from Whatcom County history; a wonderful raptors, waterfowl, and perching birds exhibit; logging industry memorabilia; an excellent firearms display; and an entire floor devoted to the works of local artists on a revolving basis. The grand old building housing all this was originally Bellingham's City Hall and dates from 1892. The Children's Museum Northwest is located just down the street, at 227 Prospect.

✻ Suquamish Museum

Suquamish Tribal Center, Suquamish (just off Highway 305, southwest of Poulsbo). 598-3311. Wednesday through Sunday, 10–4, winter; daily, 10– 5, summer. Adults $2.50; Seniors $2; children (under 12) $1.

The well-marked grave of Chief Sealth, or Seattle, is located here, with his totem and a Suquamish Indian historical museum, all near the shores of Agate Pass between the Kitsap Peninsula and Bainbridge Island. The museum is about a 15-minute drive from the Winslow ferry, you can call in advance to be picked up at the ferry terminal if you come on foot. There is a charge for this service. The museum itself, with excellent historic exhibits and audio-visual presentations, along with nearby trails and beachfront, makes this a fine day-trip destination.

The little village celebrates Chief Seattle's birthday each year in mid-August with a salmon bake, canoe races, dancing, and games.

�֎ Poulsbo Marine Museum
17771 Fjord Drive N.E., Poulsbo. 779-5549. Weekdays, 8–4, through the school year; call for summer hours and schedules of classes for children. Free.

This is a no frills marine-biology teaching center for young students and science teachers. Anytime you choose to visit you are likely to find interesting teaching and research projects. There are always plenty of display tanks filled with critters, and there is a "touch tank" if you'd like to pet a starfish or perhaps an octopus! Says one Marine Science Center enthusiast, "We're not the Seattle Aquarium, but sometimes we're more fun."

✖ Sea and Shore Museum
Port Gamble General Store, Port Gamble. 297-2426. Tuesday through Sunday, 11–4, summer; weekends, 11–4, winter. Free.

Port Gamble is among the last company-owned towns around, a property of Pope and Talbot, Inc. One of its special attractions is the Sea and Shore Museum, the work of Gamble-born Tom Rice, whose collection of mollusk shells was assembled over 30-plus years from more than 100 countries. Several thousand of the collection's 20,000 specimens are on display. Mr. Rice also edits an international, quarterly magazine for shell collectors.

Founded in 1853, Port Gamble is one of the prettiest historic villages on Puget Sound. After the General Store ("County Store") and shell museum, visit the historic museum in the building's basement. It features the history of Port Gamble and Pope and Talbot, Inc. The town's old Episcopal church is another choice bit of visible history.

✖ Skagit County Historical Museum
501 S. 4th Street, La Conner. 466-3365. Wednesday through Sunday, noon–5. Adults $1; childen (5–12) 50¢.

This charming, small museum provides a wonderful reason to visit waterside La Conner, one of Puget Sound's best main streets for walking—shops, small restaurants, junky antiques, funky art, and some serious galleries.

The museum contains attractive exhibits emphasizing the region's logging, mining, transportation, and farming industries. Among its historic treasures are an original circa 1920 Waterloo Boy tractor, a 1905 pianola, Native American displays, and turn-of-the-century household artifacts. There's also a full-scale blacksmith shop and a walk-in general store.

✴ Carnation Farm

Just outside Carnation. 788-1511. April through October, Monday through Saturday, 10–3. Closed holidays. Free.

A perennial favorite on the kids' Western Washington hit parade, the 1,000-acre estate provides city youngsters with a look at a real working dairy farm. You can tour the farm's maternity and calf barns, see milking operations, and visit some beautiful Labrador retrievers at "Friskies Acres," the estate's canine kennels. The farm also has some well-groomed flower gardens and picnic areas.

✴ Museum of Doll Art

1116 108th Avenue N.E., Bellevue. 455-1116. Monday through Wednesday, 9–5; Thursday 1–8; Friday and Saturday, 9–5; Sunday 1–5. Adults $5; children (5–17) $4.

Housed in an elegant new building near downtown Bellevue, there's something nostalgic here for almost everyone. Childhoods haunt the place in hundreds of dolls of all origins, eras, and degrees of art and artistry. Bears, toys, miniatures, and masterpieces—they're all here, from sprightly ballet dancers to John Wayne, from Winnie-the-Pooh to British royalty.

The museum boasts an excellent store which features, of course, dolls, including some frightfully expensive editions. The museum is equally "cool" for boys *and* girls.

✴ Northwest Seaport

Moss Bay Marina, 135 Lake S., Kirkland. 447-9800. Weekdays, 10–4. Free.

You'll find old classic boats here, owned and under restoration by Northwest Seaport, a nonprofit organization valiantly trying to save some of Puget Sound's maritime heritage. When you visit the lightship *Relief* and historic tugboat *Arthur Foss,* a donation is greatly appreciated by the volunteers who work on the boats. *Relief* is the last surviving steam-powered lightship in the world. *Arthur Foss* was a star in the popular Tugboat Annie films produced during the 1930s and 1940s.

✳ Hiram M. Chittenden Locks (Government Locks)

3015 N.W. 54th, Seattle. 783-7059. Daily, 7–9. Visitors Center, 10–7, summer; Thursday through Monday, 11–5, winter. Free.

Maybe the best free show in Seattle—the "locks," U.S. Army Corps of Engineers Visitors Center, adjacent fish ladders, and Carl S. English, Jr., Botanical Garden are unique, and top candidates for a family outing.

An endless progression of boats passes through the locks between Lake Washington and Puget Sound via the Lake Washington Ship Canal. The locks, by raising and lowering water levels, make up for the difference in elevations between the two bodies of water. The daily show is terrific—every kind of small boat imaginable passes through the locks, as well as some boats that are not so small. The larger of the two locks accommodates ocean-going ships and tugboats.

Next door to the locks is a fish ladder that lets migrating salmon and steelhead pass the Lake Washington Ship Canal dam. The installation includes an underwater viewing room that allows you to watch the migrating fish eye-to-eye.

The Visitors Center presents an excellent exhibit of the locks' history, including a working model of their engineering. And often overlooked in the excitement of watching migrating boats and fish are the magnificent plantings of rhododendrons and other flowering ornamentals in adjacent Carl S. English, Jr., Garden. The park is a year-round showplace, with more than 1,500 varieties of trees and shrubs from around the world. In May it's extraordinary.

✳ Seattle Art Museum

100 University Street, Seattle. 625-8901. Tuesday through Saturday, 10–5; Sunday, 12–5. Adults $6; students $4; children (under 12) free.

Big, new, and architecturally frigid, the recently opened, downtown Seattle Art Museum isn't nearly as pleasant to visit with children as its venerable counterpart in Volunteer Park, but it is bigger and presumably does a better job of organizing and displaying art. (The *old* museum, happily, will soon reopen to showcase Asian art, a specialty in the Seattle Art Museum's collection.) Watch for special exhibits here, some of which are especially well suited to young folks, and consider family memberships, which are bargains if you visit regularly. The Seattle Art Museum's collection is strong in Asian and Native American art, and includes an excellent collection of African and modern art. The gift shop is well stocked with art books, including titles for children.

✬ Museum of History and Industry

2700 24th Avenue E., Seattle. 324-1125. Monday through Saturday, 10–5; Sunday, 12–5. Adults $3; children $1.50. On Tuesdays by donation.

The emphasis here is on Seattle and Puget Sound history, with some nice displays of pioneer life and customs, and even nicer displays of historic boats and maritime history. There are hands-on attractions for children. During the holidays each year, the museum sponsors some of the community's most elegant and interesting seasonal exhibits.

A tip for young submariners: In the northeast corner of the big, downstairs exhibit room there is a working World War II periscope with which one can sight cars crossing the Evergreen Point Bridge. The standing record to beat is two Porsches, six Toyotas, and a gold Lexus.

"Down scope!"

✬ Center for Wooden Boats

(See Chapter 5)

A great place that's getting better, this hands-on museum is dedicated to the small-boat heritage of Puget Sound. All the "exhibits" are on the water for rental use. (The best time to see *all* the small boats is on Christmas, when the center is closed.) There's almost always something going on here, including classes in everything from sail making to knot tying.

The Center also provides speakers and slide shows on small boats and boat building for groups and schools.

✬ Pacific Science Center

Seattle Center. 443-2001. Daily; call for frequently changing schedules. Adults $6; children (6–13) $5; under 6 $4.

This wonderful resource for education and entertainment is without peer in the Pacific Northwest. Constantly changing exhibits emphasize "hands-on" learning when possible, and there are certain to be new surprises every time you visit. Everyone, regardless of age, will find something of fascination at the Center. Ongoing special attractions include:

The Laser Fantasy (443-2850), a remarkable, hour-long light show. You lie on your back to watch, listen, and absorb the stunning lightworks.

IMAX (443-IMAX), a large theater where shows are projected on a screen so big you feel immersed in the visual environment. It's three-stories high!

The Center's School for Science (443-2925), an ongoing program of classes and workshops tailored for students age 3 to 103. Classes are conducted afternoons, weekends, and weekdays during the summer on such subjects as basic sciences, natural history, computer science, mathematics, photography, and even magic. Average cost is about $5 per session.

The Science Center provides entertainment for everyone. For many families it's also a beloved institution of continuing education. Annual family memberships, which include discounts for events, classes, and gift-shop purchases, are $35.

Thomas Burke Memorial Museum

University of Washington, N.E. 45th and 17th Avenue N.E., Seattle. 543-5590. Daily, 10–5. Adults $3; 6–18 $1.50.

This is a classic museum of natural history, with display case after display case of neat stuff, including a dinosaur, zoology exhibits, fossils, rocks and minerals, shells, and Coast Indian arts and crafts. There's appropriate emphasis on the Pacific Northwest and Pacific Rim; an excellent collection of Coast Indian artifacts for the enjoyment of both young anthropologists and professional scientists; hands-on activities for kids of all ages; and an excellent museum shop.

Nordic Heritage Museum

3014 N.W. 67th, Seattle. 789-5707. Tuesday through Saturday, 10–4; Sunday, 12–4. Adults (over 16) $2.50; children $1.

This is a special place for the many Northwesterners of Scandinavian ancestry and a warm cultural museum for anyone with an interest in immigrant life in America. There is a "touch" display of hats reflecting different occupations—farming, fishing, logging, and even Sunday-go-to-meeting. And there are handcrafted items, including boats, tools, kitchen utensils, clothing, and costumes.

Coast Guard Museum of the Northwest

Pier 36, Seattle. 286-9608. Monday, Wednesday, Friday, 10–4; weekends, 1–5. Free.

This small museum is dedicated to the U.S. Coast Guard in the Pacific Northwest and is a nice reminder of just how important the Coast Guard is to both commerce and recreation on Washington's marine waterways. It contains some wonderful ship's models, past and present; marine artifacts and old photographs; and considerable information about the Coast Guard's lighthouse system. A visit here may be all the richer if there's a grandad or two along to put some of the history on display into perspective.

Next door to the museum, all this comes to life in the Coast Guard Vessel Traffic Center, open daily from 8 to 4.

✳ Ye Olde Curiosity Shop

Pier 54, Seattle. 682-5844. Daily, 9:30–6; Friday and Saturday, 9–9. Free.

Most parents avoid "souvenir shops" like the measles, but this place is one-of-a-kind and magnificent in its own fashion, if patently commercial. From some remarkable Native American artifacts to the craziest junk you've ever seen, this is the shop with something for absolutely everyone. In business since 1899, the store has become an internationally famous landmark in Seattle, with lots of NFS (not for sale) items to look at along with thousands of other things to buy and call your own. Among the NFS attractions are two mummies, a handful of shrunken heads, some wicked, if fanciful, knives, swords, and firearms, and the Lord's Prayer engraved on a grain of rice.

Children will find things to fit modest budgets such as coins, post-cards, seashells, small toys, bits of magic, stuffed critters (both real and imaginary), flags, feathers, rings, hats—the list goes on and on.

✳ Klondike Gold Rush National Historic Park

117 S. Main, Seattle. 553-7220. Daily, 9–5. Free.

This is the Seattle unit of a National Historic Park that has locations in Alaska, British Columbia, and the Yukon Territory. In 1897, gold discoveries in the Yukon set off a stampede of would-be prospectors that lured 100,000 people north, many of them by way of Seattle, where they bought their "grubstakes" for the odyssey north. The gold rush of 1897–98 is preserved here in old photographs and memorabilia, including the classic comedy film "The Gold Rush," starring Charlie Chaplin. The exhibits and presentations are beautifully orchestrated with the National Park Service's characteristic attention to detail.

✳ Seattle Children's Museum

Seattle Center (Center House). 441-1767. Tuesday through Sunday, 10–5. For children, 2–10 (children must be accompanied by an adult). $3.50 per person; under 1 free.

A unique, absolutely hands-on place for children and parents to play and "work" together in such activities as role-playing and exploring

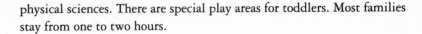

physical sciences. There are special play areas for toddlers. Most families stay from one to two hours.

✳ Wing Luke Museum
407 7th Avenue S., Seattle. 623-5124. Tuesday through Friday, 11–4:30; weekends, 12–4. Adults $2.50; children 75¢.

Dedicated to preserving and interpreting Asian culture, this museum is named for a popular Seattle city councilman who died in a small-plane crash in 1965. It contains old photographs and cultural items ranging from fans to firecrackers. Special exhibits are changed about every two months, and there is an ongoing program of classes in Asian folk arts and crafts.

Located in Seattle's International District, a visit to the museum provides a good reason to try one of the neighborhood's several Chinese restaurants for a "dim sum" lunch. The many kinds of dim sum (tea cakes, or "touch the heart," a rough translation) are snack-like delicacies you select from food carts; your empty dishes are counted to compute your bill. Kids love running up the bill!

✳ Underground Seattle
Doc Maynard's Public House, 1st Avenue and James Street, Seattle. 682-4646. Daily, on the hour, 11 to 4 or 5. Adults $5.50; youths $4; children (6–12) $2.25. Reservations recommended.

These 90-minute historic tours of "underground Seattle" are rich in turn-of-the-century anecdotes. The "underground" portion of the tour takes you through the basements of the buildings in Pioneer Square that were at street level in the 1890s. The street level was raised a story in the reconstruction following Seattle's devastating fire of 1889. The tour begins in a saloon, restored to its 1890s glory, and ends at a Pioneer Square gift shop. This is a walker's tour, best reserved for older children.

✳ Museum of Flight
9404 E. Marginal Way S., Seattle. 764-5720. Adults $5; teens $3; youths $2; under 6 free.

The two things that make this museum extraordinary are its exhibits and docents. In the six-story steel and glass Great Gallery about half of the airplanes on exhibit are in the air, including a suspended DC-3! There's a replica of the Wright brothers' original glider and the first Air Force F-5 supersonic fighter. There's United Airlines' first mail plane, a 1929 Boeing 18-passenger tri-motor, and a fully-restored World War II

Corsair fighter. You can walk right up to a Blue Angels jet and much, much more.

The volunteer museum staff are as interesting as the exhibits. Not surprisingly in the city that's home to Boeing Corporation, there is some real expertise on hand, but it is the enthusiasm of the docents that contributes so much to the museum experience. Linger over a plane too long and you may well hear, "She's a beauty, isn't she? I flew that plane in the Pacific."

Not all the docents are pilots or engineers, but they can all talk about airplanes by the hour. The amazing thing is you can easily listen to them by the hour.

A caution to moms: It's the rare son who doesn't contract the urge to be a pilot on a visit to the Museum of Flight. Daughters can catch the contagion, too. And dads are worst of all.

✳ Pioneer Farm

Three miles north of Eatonville, in Ohop Valley, via either State Highway 7 from Tacoma or State Highway 161 from Puyallup. 832-6300. Weekends, 11–5; daily, Father's Day to Labor Day. Call for group information. Adults $5; children $4.

The guided one-and-one-half-hour tour is just an introduction to this step back into the Pacific Northwest a century ago. Young visitors live the past, wearing pioneer clothes and doing the chores pioneers did to work and live on the land. Children are introduced to building log houses and barns, blacksmithing, woodworking, and farmyard chores. Even more ambitious are day-long programs for organized groups, in which youngsters really roll up their sleeves and totally immerse themselves in the past.

Also visit the Ohop Indian Village, open weekends through the summer. At 1 and 2:30 there are hands-on living history tours that let children try centuries-old, Native American skills and crafts.

✳ Camp Six (Western Washington Forest Museum)

In Point Defiance Park, Tacoma (see Chapter 1). 752-0047.

Here's an outdoor museum that reflects the history of Western Washington's logging industry clear back to 1800. It's a treasure. On display is the last Lidgerwood skidder left in the world, all 666,000 pounds of it. In its heyday it required a crew of 17 men. There's a John Dolbeer Steam Donkey from 1869, on loan from the Smithsonian Institution, and, the kids' favorite, a Shay Number 7 steam locomotive. Actually, the Shay was originally Number 2, but one of its early day engineers renamed it for his favorite brand of whiskey, Seagram's 7. There are other steam-donkey engines, a spar pole, and yarders. Three of the Camp Six bunk houses contain antique logging photographs, equipment, and tools. The site is on the National Register of Historic Places. It's open Labor Day to Memorial Day, 11 to 6.

✳ Fort Nisqually

In Point Defiance Park, Tacoma (see Chapter 1).

Fort Nisqually was established in 1833 by the Hudson's Bay Company. Restored buildings from the original outpost include the stockade, trading store, granary, and blacksmith shop, all well stocked with tools and relics of the mid-1880s. A rich collection of pioneer artifacts and household items is on display at the Fort Nisqually Museum, open daily, noon to 6, summer; Tuesday through Sunday, 1 to 4, winter.

✳ The Nature Center at Snake Lake

1919 S. Tyler, Tacoma. 591-6439. Daily, 8–dusk. Free.

You can walk a mile-long nature trail by yourself, or call for information about guided tours that offer absorbing introductions to the natural history of the area. There are dozens of stopping places along the trails (two and one-half miles of trails in total), well-described in the center's self-guiding brochure available at the interpretive nature center and shop.

Wonderful classes for children are offered and range from decorating with natural materials to Christmas for animals.

✳ Fort Lewis Military Museum

Fort Lewis. Exit 119 off Interstate 5, near Dupont. 967-7206. Tuesday through Sunday, noon–4. Free.

This military historical museum has treasures that include paintings of the 1804–1805 Lewis and Clark Expedition. But most of the uniforms, weapons, and Indian artifacts date from the Civil War period to the present, with emphasis on Northwest military history, and the histories of the First Army Corps and Ninth Infantry Division.

Warriors of all ages enjoy the outdoor motorpool of tanks and armored combat vehicles, including some returned from action in the Gulf War.

✳ State Capitol Museum

211 W. 21st Avenue, Olympia. 753-2580. Tuesday through Friday, 10–4; weekends, 12–4. $5 donation suggested for families.

This 1922 mansion contains some excellent exhibits of Indian and pioneer artifacts, art, history, and Washington State and Territorial memorabilia. The beautiful grounds contain a Pioneer Herb Garden and a Native Plant Garden. Special exhibits change every six to eight weeks. The museum sponsors a varied program of classes and events for both children and adults.

�֍ State Capitol Tours

State Capitol, Olympia. 586-8687. Daily, 10–3. Free.

These 45-minute tours are fascinating for schoolchildren. They offer a sampling of history, civics, and, if the legislature is in session, a few minutes of legislative rhetoric.

On Wednesdays the Governor's Mansion is open for tours. Call 586-8687.

✖ Capitol Conservatory

State Capitol grounds, Olympia. 586-8687. Daily, 10–3. Free.

This is the greenhouse and horticultural gardens where the plants and flowers for the capitol buildings are grown. The gardens are enjoyable year round and are quite spectacular in late spring.

8

Exploring Afoot

Young children don't care much for urban walking tours unless they include a lot of interesting things to see and do—without walking long distances to get there. Seattle Center, Pioneer Square in Seattle, and La Conner farther north all meet these requirements. The following roundup includes some of the region's classics. Most of these are commercially oriented, with many kinds of foods, sweets, retail displays of toys, handcrafts, souvenirs, collectibles, and other temptations. *Caveat pater.*

✸ Port Townsend
At the tip of its own peninsula, where the Strait of Juan de Fuca meets Admiralty Inlet to Puget Sound.

Port Townsend may be a little too Victorian for toddlers, but it's the premier place to "view" history in Western Washington. Its founders anticipated it would be the territory's first city. It didn't quite live up to expectations, but today its 19th-century village environment provides a rich architectural portfolio of living history.

You can't possibly walk all of it, but pick up a map at the Visitor Information Center at Sims Way and Kearney Street. A small business district runs along Water Street next to the waterfront, with some arts and crafts shops, restaurants, and cafes on the retail levels of several old brick business buildings. The residential community, where the town's picture-postcard Victorian houses are located, is up the hill from the business section and best toured by car.

For a family picnic and lawns for playing, head for Fort Warden, now a state park. Duplexes in the old officers' row are available for rent; make reservations in advance. Nearby Point Wilson Lighthouse, built in 1879, is open to visitors Wednesday through Friday, 1 to 3; weekends, 1 to 4.

✸ La Conner
Seventy miles north of Seattle, 20 minutes from Interstate 5, exit 221.

This old fishing village has evolved into a funky, artsy-craftsy community, with boutiques, small restaurants, galleries, antiques shops—something to satisfy almost every interest. Most of the antique stores see you coming; don't expect bargains. But they are of less interest to children than the places selling souvenirs, seashells, and culinary treats.

The boat watching is terrific. The waterside portion of main street is built on creaking old piers over Swinomish Slough, a pokey, narrow waterway, heavily traveled by small boats, from yachts to trawlers. There is the Skagit County Historical Museum to visit (see Chapter 7) and a Volunteer Firemen Museum. Pioneer Park, just south of town, has a nice playground and picnic areas.

✴ Coupeville

Midway up Whidbey Island on Penn Cove, via State Highway 525 from the Clinton Ferry Terminal (Mukilteo Ferry).

Downtown Coupeville is a historic treasure with Victorian residences dating from 1852. You can obtain a walking-tour map at the Island County Historical Museum, open 1 to 4:30, Sunday through Thursday; 10:30 to 4:30, Friday and Saturday. The museum displays an exceptional collection of Indian baskets. Twenty-six old houses are located in the Central Whidbey Historic District.

Mariner's Court is a mall of shops and restaurants, including The Honey Bear, which sells all kinds of teddy bears and, what else—candy jars. There are antique stores, galleries, and some interesting places to lunch or snack. The Knead & Feed restaurant overlooks sleepy Penn Cove and specializes in freshly baked goods.

✴ Seattle Center

Bounded by Denny Way, Mercer Street, 1st Avenue N., and 5th Avenue N. 684-7200.

This 74-acre legacy from the 1962 Seattle World's Fair is not only in the heart of the city, but in the hearts of Seattle residents as well. It serves as the city's cultural center, entertainment capital, and a world-class rainy day refuge. It's home of the Pacific Science Center (see Chapter 7), but that's just the beginning. Here you'll find the 520-foot-high Space Needle, with its observation deck and restaurant (expensive); Center House (see Chapter 10), with small food bars and cafes serving international temptations, including a wide variety of sweets and ice creams; a Fun Forest amusement park with all kinds of rides; the Pacific Arts Center, showcasing performing and fine arts of young people; and several beautiful, large fountains, so resplendent they attract crowds to watch the performances of water and lights. The Center's handsome campus is also home of Seattle's Opera House, a theater, and an auditorium/ice arena. All are within easy walking distance of each other.

The Seattle Center Monorail carries passengers on an elevated mono track to downtown Seattle at Westlake Mall. It is a delightful 90-second ride, worth the 80-cent fare just for the sightseeing. It's also a practical way to park your car at Seattle Center, where there is abundant parking, and explore the downtown area. Monorail hours: 10 to midnight, Sunday through Thursday; 10 to half-past midnight, weekends.

✴ Seattle Waterfront

Pier 48 to Pier 70, roughly from the foot of Jackson Street to Stewart Street.

This long stretch of Seattle's waterfront has emerged from the city's many miles of commercial and industrial footage as a prime recreational area on Puget Sound. It's adjacent to downtown and close to several major hotels. When the legs grow weary, you can catch the Waterfront Trolley, an old streetcar that runs from Broad Street to Main Street. The fare is 60 cents, and you may get on and off just about as you please.

Ye Olde Curiosity Shop at Pier 54 (see Chapter 7) is a good reason to visit the waterfront. Nearby is the Washington State Ferries headquarters and the ferry docks for Bremerton and Winslow. Firehouse 5, next to Pier 54, is the home of the fireboats *Alki* and *Duwamish*. During summer weekends the fireboats pull out into Elliott Bay to spray an awesome amount of water into the air. Past a ship's chandlery is Seattle Harbor Tours headquarters at Pier 56. They also arrange daily trips to Blake Island for an Indian-style salmon bake at Tillicum Village.

Moving along past a public fishing pier, the Seattle Aquarium (Chapter 1), and B.C. Ferry's headquarters for *Princess Marguerite* (with summer trips daily to Victoria and back), you pass still more shops and restaurants until you reach Pier 70, a complex of specialty stores and places to snack or dine.

There is parking near the waterfront along the way, but its availability in summer is chancy; best near Pier 70, with its nearby parking garage.

From the Seattle Waterfront it is an easy two-block hike up to Pike Place Market or a few blocks over to Pioneer Square, but beware of trying to tackle all three destinations or even two of them in one outing if you have young children in tow. Combined, they represent quite a lot of walking.

✴ Pike Place Market

At the foot of Pike Street, one block from 1st Avenue, Seattle. Monday through Saturday, 9–6.

Like Pioneer Square, Pike Place Market is a true social melting pot, earthy, alive, and full of fun. It's deservedly a candidate for Seattle's number one tourist attraction, yet it is still the favorite place for many Seattle residents to buy their produce, meats, and seafoods. Everything—the fruits and vegetables, crabs and fish, fresh baked breads—looks outstanding in the public market. Entirely covered, it's a perfect walking tour for a rainy day.

In the market itself and across the street you'll find dozens of specialty food shops, along with small variety stores, some of them with great appeal to children. Tops on the kids' hit parade is Golden Age Collectibles, specializing in comic books, vintage posters, and radio broadcast recordings. There's also the Wonderful Wooden Toy Shop, The Magic Shop, and The Poppery, with a thousand different kinds of candies from around the world. And don't miss The Cookie Jar and The Chocolate Factory. All great fun, but none of them endorsed by the American Dental Association.

One of the market's great appeals is the large area reserved for street vendors to display their wares. Many vendors sell works of art, weavings, and handcrafts. Toymakers offer unusual playthings here, from hand-carved, wooden kaleidoscopes to tops and kites.

✴ Pioneer Square

Roughly between Yesler Way and S. King Street; the waterfront and 2nd Avenue, Seattle.

This 12-square-block area is the heart of old Seattle, restored in recent years to something of its former rough-hewn elegance. Yesler Way was the original "Skid Road" (named for a sawmill log skid and often misnamed "skid row"), and parents should be forewarned that there are still a few old-timers here in spirit(s). But the area also contains a wonderful assortment of art galleries, some unique shops, an assortment of places to eat, bookstores, and even a glassblowing factory. More than 100 interesting places are listed on walking-tour maps widely distributed by Pioneer Square merchants.

In addition to the Klondike Gold Rush National Historic Park (see Chapter 7) there are several places of special interest to youngsters: Magic Mouse Toys, 217 1st S., which sells quality toys from around the world, "selected by a professional child," including dolls and wooden trains; The Wood Shop, 402 Occidental S., described as a "cross between a toymaker's workshop, a gift shop, and a zoo"; Great Winds Kite Shop, 166 S. Jackson, with a worldwide assortment of kites, from $2 to $350; The Iron Horse Restaurant, 311 3rd S., where model trains deliver burgers and sandwiches to your table; and Seattle Toy Company, 110 Alaskan Way S., situated in an old firehouse, with both new and antique toys.

Reservations are a must for the tours of Underground Seattle beneath the existing street level (see Chapter 7).

✯ Volunteer Park

15th Avenue E. and E. Galer Street, Seattle.

Seattle has many delightful parks. Volunteer Park is the oldest and has a lion's share of surprises, all within easy walking distance of each other. The Seattle Art Museum's main branch is now located downtown (see Chapter 7), but the original museum building remains here as an annex. There's a big greenhouse conservatory, a water tower (with a sweeping view from the top), attractive playgrounds, and lovely gardens that dazzle in late spring. The park's wading pool for children is filled only on warm days during summer. It's a Seattle institution; generations of local kids have splashed and played here.

9

Mountain Trails and Expeditions

Many a wise parent will simply ignore this category of family activity, knowing from experience that following the trail of Lewis and Clark with kids is every bit as perilous as crossing hostile Indian country in tornado weather with provisions running low. What is the appeal, anyway, of slogging up a mountain path with a mutinous mob who would gleefully abandon you for the promise of a cold Coke and a pizza?

If there's an answer required, it probably rests in the fact that Western Washington has the market cornered on the world's loveliest mountains. Sure, Europe boasts the Alps, but they don't hold a candle to the North Cascades. California has the Sierra, but the Sierra doesn't have a Mt. Rainier, a Baker, an Adams, or a St. Helens. A lot of places have mountain ranges, but few can match the Olympics for photogenic elegance. Best of all, the Puget Sound region's mountains are nearby, providing hundreds of trails and routes just minutes away. Nowhere else in the conterminous United States can you proceed from metropolitan city center to mountain wilderness so fast.

Happily, all these mountains and trails support a thriving guidebook industry: trail guides, walkers' guides, climbing guides, backpacking guides, bicycling guides, backroad guides, nature guides, and guides that review the guides. Many of them are delightful adventures in reading as well as being useful and informative. An amazing number of these comprehensive trail guides are published by the Mountaineers; the organization also conducts outings for members, ranging from day walks to expeditionary winter climbs. A note to The Mountaineers, 300 Third Avenue W., Seattle, WA 98119, will get you a catalog of their publications and family membership information.

The hikes recommended here are selected from hundreds of possibilities. They do not require much uphill walking (with a couple of noted exceptions), and they are among Washington's most magnificent day walks, which means they are world class.

To be sure, some children are more keen on hiking than others. A leisurely pace, a couple of field guides, a pair of binoculars, and a magnifying glass will enrich a mountain walk for everyone. On the other hand, it's not unusual to see families on what appear to be forced marches on

Washington trails. They'll typically overtake you in full song—yodeling, bellowing "I am a happy wanderer," whistling, things of that kind.

To veterans of backcountry trails it's a litany as shopworn as airline safety instructions and no less important; here it is again. Even during a short trail walk in Western Washington, weather can turn unexpectedly, and so can a knee or an ankle. Hypothermia—the chilling of body temperature from exposure to cold and wet weather—is a serious, but easily avoidable, danger year round. Always carry the essentials:

- Extra clothing, including rain gear
- Extra food
- Sunglasses (a must for snowy, high alpine country)
- Knife (for first aid, emergency fire building)
- First aid kit (with sun screen, lip balm)
- Waterproof matches and candle or chemical firestarter
- Small flashlight (with extra bulb and batteries)
- Map (of your hiking area)
- Compass
- A daypack or rucksack to carry the above

For little kids, one of the several children's backpack carriers will enlarge your range. Small children will even nap in the packs, and some of the packs contain an extra pocket or two to carry some or all of the above essentials.

✳ Chain of Lakes/Ptarmigan Ridge
State Highway 542 to road end in Heather Meadows Recreation Area. Mt. Baker National Forest. 442-5400. USGS Maps "Mt. Shuksan" and "Mt. Baker."

Heather Meadows is near the Canadian border and a long haul from Seattle/Tacoma, but for breathtaking mountain scenery it's the staging area for trail systems without peer. The Chain of Lakes Loop is a six-mile hike on the vigorous side (about a 1,500-foot elevation gain), and the Ptarmigan Ridge Trail is often described, in grave tones, as a climber's approach to Mt. Baker, which it is. Throughout this alpine country summer comes late and ends early, with August and early September usually providing the best snow-free window for day hiking.

For a mostly level, stunning round-trip walk of about three miles that's easily negotiated *when snowfree*, follow the Chain of Lakes Trail from the west side of Kulshan Ridge road-end parking area for one mile to the saddle between Ptarmigan Ridge and Table Mountain. From here you can walk another half-mile or so down the Ptarmigan Ridge Trail before the talus enlarges to small boulders and snow fields block the way.

In the mountainous scheme of things you stroll between Mt. Baker and Mt. Shuksan, each looming above you and displaying themselves in all their craggy, snowy, awesome alpine splendor. Besides the climbers you'll see on the trail—bedecked with ice axes, crampons, ropes, and carabiners—you may encounter artists packing easels and paints, along with gaggles of photographers. You do not need to cover great distances here to enjoy the mountain scenery, nor will you want to with young children in tow, but no one will soon forget the "adventure," and all the walking is just about level from the parking area to the Ptarmigan/Table Mountain saddle.

Experienced hikers with older children might consider the entire Chain of Lakes Loop. From the Ptarmigan/Table Mountain saddle the trail descends past four sparkling glacial lakes and then back up to the Kulshan Ridge parking area, or, by using two cars, you can walk out past the Bagley Lakes to the Mt. Baker Lodge parking area, downhill all the way.

Trail and snow conditions vary vastly from year to year, so check with the Forest Service in advance of your trip to the Mt. Baker region. This alpine area is so spectacular that the advance planning and preparation are well worth the effort. Clear weather, too, is a requirement, or your "mountain adventure" will end up a cloud walk.

✳ Baker River/Sulphide Creek

Fourteen miles east of Sedro-Woolley on State Highway 20, turn left on Baker Lake–Grandy Lake Road. Proceed 14 miles to Komo Lake Guard Station on Baker Lake. Take the Forest Service Road 11 miles to the lake head and turn left .5 miles on a spur road and right on the first side road for another .5 miles to the start of Upper Baker trail No. 606. Mt. Baker National Forest/North Cascades National Park. 442-5400/856-5700. USGS maps "Lake Shannon," "Mt. Shuksan," "Mt. Challenger."

The six-mile round-trip walk to Sulphide Creek is near level and takes you into one of the choicest rain forest valleys in North Cascades National Park. Less than 1,000 feet in elevation, the trail is open spring through fall, and it's just as enjoyable on a rainy day (appropriately dressed) as when the sun's out. This is virgin forest, among the last remnants of low elevation, old-growth forest left in the Cascades, and a good place to give children a perspective on the continuing controversy about whether the last of the virgin forests should be felled. Those tag ends of old-growth forest not presently accorded National Park status in

Washington are about as secure as a chicken on a fox farm. You actually begin this walk in a National Forest (U.S. Department of Agriculture) and hike into a National Park (U.S. Department of the Interior). Along the Baker River you'll see beaver ponds, deep brooding groves of moss-mantled fir, spruce, and vine maples, views of glaciated 7,660-foot Mt. Blum, and peek-a-boo glimpses of icy peaks. It's easy walking all the way to Sulphide Creek, where you can picnic in view of Jagged Ridge.

✵ Cascade Pass

Twenty-five miles east of Marblemount on the Cascade River Road. North Cascades National Park. 856-5700. USGS map "Cascade Pass."

This is not an easy hike for small children. It's 7 miles, round trip, with an 1,800-foot elevation gain. However, the grade is gentle (32 switchbacks), and from July through early October this is the quintessential North Cascades scenic hike. Safely across a canyon from the trail, hanging glaciers continuously break off 8,200-foot Mt. Johannesburg with accompanying sound effects that echo down the canyon. Watch closely, for you can see the falling icefalls before you hear them.

At every switchback the alpine scenery becomes more astonishing and grand. Cascade Pass has probably been the subject of more published hyperbole than any other mountain trail in the Pacific Northwest...yet none of the superlatives quite capture the magic of the place.

If your hike brings you to the pass with energy to spare, you can walk another two miles along flowery Sahale Arm to enjoy the views of Doubtful Lake and Stehekin River Valley below.

✵ Tonga Ridge/Mt. Sawyer

From Skykomish, drive 1.8 miles on U.S. Highway 2 to Foss River Road; turn right, continuing on the main road (stay to the right at 1.2 miles) for 3.6 miles to Tonga Road; turn right, continuing for 7 miles; turn right on Road Number 6830-310 for 1.5 miles to the road end. Mt. Baker–Snoqualmie National Forest. 856-5700. USGS map "Scenic."

It's a 6.5-mile round-trip hike to Tonga Pass, with a climb of only about 400 feet. The trail starts some 200 feet from the road end, via Fire Trail, and takes you through a fir forest up to a ridge of flowery alpine meadows, and on to Sawyer Pass at an elevation of 4,800 feet. This is another high-country, July through September walk with magnificent mountain scenery. After the snows have melted in late summer, a bushwhack to the top of 5,500-foot Mt. Sawyer is perfectly achievable, and in late August you can pick huckleberries along the way.

From the summit of Mt. Sawyer you'll see a host of peaks, including Rainier, Baker, Glacier, Hinman, and Daniel.

✵ Mt. Si

From Interstate 90, take exit 30 to North Bend Way for about a mile; turn left on 432nd N.E. (Stilson Road), cross the river and turn right at the first intersection on Mt. Si Road; drive two miles to the Mt. Si Trailhead parking lot, on the left. Mt. Si Preservation Area. USGS maps "Mt. Si," "Snoqualmie," "North Bend," "Bandera."

If popularity counts, this is the family hike to end all. On just about any weekend, spring through fall, you are apt to encounter kids, families, boy scouts, joggers, even dogs, all trudging up the 8-mile roundtrip trail to the top of Mt. Si. This is no cake walk, but you can bite it off in attractive round-trip segments of 2 and 3.5 miles. One of the reasons for its popularity, of course, is that it is close to Seattle. Another is that it's open almost year round. The views along the trail and from the top are very nice, although increasingly more urban and suburban (you can see all the way to downtown Seattle). It may be, too, that a lot of hikers simply enjoy the pleasure of human companionship.

The elevation gain all the way to the top is 3,500 feet, which makes it a good early-season 8-mile conditioning hike. Viewpoints at one mile and at 1.75 miles make good turnaround points when hiking with children.

✵ Trail of the Shadows

Trailhead is across the road from the hotel in Longmire, Rainier National Park (Nisqually Entrance). 569-2211.

This is a .75-mile, self-guiding nature loop through an area of mineral springs and marsh, past beaver ponds and a historic log cabin, and into some lovely deep woods. It's a pleasant, informative 30-minute walk, nicely suited to the attention spans of young children, and it's a good introduction to some of the park's natural history. Although Rainier National Park's nominal focus is Mt. Rainier itself, the park contains a wealth of forest trails, lakes, streams, and volcanic thermal places of interest.

✵ Gobblers Knob

One mile inside the Nisqually Entrance to Rainier National Park, turn left and drive seven miles to Round Pass and the trailhead. 569-2211.

This is a gradual climb on a mile of trail (2 miles, round trip) to Lake George, a popular and easily reached picnic and fishing spot. It's another 1.5 miles to Gobblers Knob (5 miles, round trip), with a fairly steep climb. Gobblers Knob is a lovely alpine garden of gnarled firs, heathers, seasonal wildflowers, and an amazing face-to-face view of Mt. Rainier. The awesome peak is just across the canyon and above you here, all 14,410 feet of it. You can also see the tops of St. Helens, Adams, and Hood. Most years the trail is snowfree July through October.

✴ Green Lake

Trailhead is from Ranger Creek crossing, three miles from the Carbon River Entrance to Rainier National Park. 569-2211.

This 4-mile round trip to lovely Green Lake and back is another forest gem, with magical rain forest root formations, carpets of ferns, and—we're almost certain—leprechauns, fairy queens, and perhaps even unicorns. The entire Carbon River Valley is a superb example of low elevation, Western Cascades rain forest, one of the few to have escaped the logging pressures of the past 45 years. There is a .5-mile nature loop at the Carbon River Entrance to the Park, and several other short trails in the area that are free of snow from May through October or even later.

✴ Grove of the Patriarchs

From the Ohanapecosh River Bridge parking area, .25 mile from the Stevens Canyon Entrance to Rainier National Park. 569-2211.

This 1.5-mile loop takes you across a suspension bridge to an island in the Ohanapecosh River where Douglas firs, spruce, and cedars have been protected from fire for 1,000 years or more. There are some 30 trees over 25 feet in circumference, and a Douglas fir that's 35 feet! The largest Western Red Cedar in the park grows here. These trees were thriving here before the United States was a nation; before Columbus "discovered" America; before the first saw log was felled into Puget Sound.

10

Fun Parks and Kid Places

A vast industry is devoted to entertaining children, and although Puget Sound doesn't have a Disneyland, there are plenty of sophisticated places dedicated to amusing kids. There are also less spectacular gems like the free Mercer Island Children's Park that possibly offers the best in both pre-school childhood amusements and creative, low-budget park design.

As for parks in general, anywhere there's a bit of second-growth forest with some tree stumps and logs you have a ready-made park in Western Washington. But some have been developed with special attention to the needs and interests of youngsters.

The following is a mix of places to delight young children.

✠ Semiahmoo County Park

On Semiahmoo Parkway at the south end of Semiahmoo Spit, across Drayton Harbor from Blaine. 371-5513. Dawn to dusk.

This small Whatcom County park is a gem for children, with swimming, beachcombing, exceptional bird watching, and even some clam digging. The park has a small but excellent museum that focuses on the history and natural history of Drayton Harbor and Semiahmoo Spit, which was previously the site of one of the largest salmon canning operations in the world. The rest of the spit is now a resort development and the little park is dwarfed among golf links, condominiums, hotel, and yachts.

In summer the extreme tides of shallow Drayton Harbor expose expanses of tideland gravels to the sun; when the tides return the waters are warmed, leaving the shallow areas perfect for children to wade and swim in. If you call in advance or have a tide table, you can time your visit for a high-tide swim.

There are picnic tables at the park, and the picturesque beaches along the spit are a delight to explore. You'll likely see ospreys, bald eagles, and blue herons in the area, along with flocks of shorebirds and, in spring and fall, migrating waterfowl. Deer, attracted by the water and irrigated fairways of the Semiahmoo golf course, are frequently seen along the parkway.

�֎ Lake Serene Pony Farm

3915 Serene Way, Lynnwood. 743-2112. Saturday. $5 per ride for ages 3–14. Call for appointment.

With indoor and outdoor picnic areas, a ghost town that you enter through a tree stump, and gentle horses to ride, this is a choice outing designed just for young children. The farm offers a special summer program during which children can "own" a horse for a week. Ownership includes feeding and grooming, along with learning to ride and special riding events.

✶ Gold Creek Trout Farm

15844 148th N.E., Woodinville. 483-1415. Daily, 10–5. You pay for the fish you catch, by size. A 10-inch fish is $1.95

There's no doubt that the devil created trout farms to delight children and bankrupt parents. Here's a wonderful place for small kids (and big kids) where they'll be assured of catching fish. The farm provides poles and bait, everything you need. The trout are priced according to their size. The hatchery-raised fish are delicious and about the same price you'd pay for them at a fish market, plus you have the fun of catching them yourself. Set a limit on the catch and it's great fun. The fish are cleaned and wrapped for you at no extra cost. Large groups should call for reservations.

✶ Mercer Island Children's Park

Next to Island Park School on Island Crest Way at 54th S.E. Daily, dawn to dusk. Free.

On sunny days, this is a veritable garden of earthly delights for pre-schoolers, with some fanciful play and climbing devices scaled to their size, rain forest paths, and peaceful picnic tables. It is damp and dark on cloudy days.

✶ Kelsey Creek Park

At the end of S.E. 4th Place, Bellevue. 455-7688. Dawn to dusk (the farm animals receive visitors, 7–4). Free.

Kelsey Creek Park is no secret, but getting there is. This wonderful facility is artfully concealed in a quiet suburban neighborhood in Bellevue; locating the park can be a terror (see below for directions). Bellevue residents just three blocks away may not know how to direct you.

Among the park's attractions for kids are an animal farm with sheep, goats, ponies, cows, pigs, rabbits, chickens, ducks, and, in the spring mostly, lambs, kids, calves, shoats, colts, bunnies, and chicks. It's a close-up and hands-on demonstration farm, immaculately groomed. It's especially delightful for little "city kids." And there is a play area, too, for small children.

There are also walking paths through a semi-formal Japanese garden that is bisected by Kelsey Creek, and there is a superb three-quarter-mile nature loop through mixed woods with excellent signage.

In October you may see migrating salmon in Kelsey Creek, and the small stream is home for mallard ducks year round. There are picnic tables in several areas of the park, including along the nature trail.

How to get there: From Interstate 405 in Bellevue, take exit 13 to S.E. 8th Street. Proceed east under the railroad trestle (where N.E. 8th becomes 132nd Place S.E.). At the intersection with the Lake Hills Connector keep straight. The road turns right, then left, then straightens to become S.E. 7th. At a stop sign, turn left onto 128th Ave. S.E., then right onto S.E. 4th Place. Drive two blocks to the park entrance and parking lot.

✴ Marymoor Park
6064 W. Lake Sammamish Parkway N.E., Redmond. 885-3684. Daily, dawn to dusk. Free.

A quintessential suburban park on Sammamish Slough that's complete with play fields, picnic areas, swings and play sets, tennis courts, a jogging track, and a museum. The museum contains historical displays from the "eastside communities" of Bellevue, Redmond, and Kirkland, including room settings. This is a great family park. Even dogs are welcome.

✴ Puget Sound and Snoqualmie Valley Railroad
State Highway 202, downtown Snoqualmie. 888-3030 or 746-4025. Weekends, 11–5, summer; Sunday, 11–3:30, spring. Special seasonal schedules. Adults $5; children (5–11) $3; under 5 free.

With 10 miles of track between Snoqualmie and North Bend, this is a wonderful rail tour for everyone, especially in the company of nostalgic rail buffs. There are special holiday trains: a "spook train" in October and a Santa Claus train in December. You can also catch the train in North Bend. It's a one-hour-and-twenty-minute rail trip.

✴ Lil' Bit O'Heaven
16636 N.E. 40th, Redmond. 883-1654. Daily, 9:30–5; closed Tuesday and Saturday. You pay for the fish you catch, from $2.25 for a 9-incher and up at 50 cents per inch.

With park-like grounds, a good place for little kids to catch trout. There are benches for brown-bag picnics.

✳ Springbrook Trout Farm

19225 Talbot Road S., Renton. 852-0360. March through October, daily, 10–dusk. Closed winter. You pay for the fish you catch.

An attractive, well-managed trout farm with picnic areas and some very large fish! The small fish ponds are recommended for youngsters. If the budget's no problem there are also some large hybrid trout to be caught here, fish in the five-pound-and-up category. For groups of 12 or more, call for reservations. Families may drop by anytime. Everything (including cleaning the fish) is provided. The fish you catch cost just about what you'd pay at a fish market.

✳ Can-Mar Trout Farm

288633 216th Avenue S.E., Kent. 630-4912. January through October, weekends 10–dusk; Monday though Friday by appointment. Whatever you catch is $3.35 a pound.

The trout farm has two well-stocked ponds from which you may extract fish either with your own tackle or with cane poles, lines, and baited hooks supplied by the management. It's not the Montana of "A River Runs Through It," but one occasionally sees a fly fisherman here "practicing" his art.

✳ Gene Coulon Memorial Beach Park (Lake Washington Park)

Renton, at the southern end of Lake Washington (see Chapter 4).

An excellent family park complex with a large covered cooking and picnic area, a play fort with climbing tower, a fully-equipped playground, volleyball and tennis courts, shuffleboard, horseshoe pits, and a swimming beach (with a lifeguard during summer). You'll also find small-boat launching and food concessions. And lots of ducks to feed.

This is an award-winning park campus, with something for everyone. Kite flying is prohibited because of nearby high-power lines.

✳ Seattle Children's Museum

Seattle Center, Center House (see Chapter 7). 441-1767. Tuesday through Sunday, 10–5. $3.50; under 1 free.

A unique, absolutely hands-on play place for children and parents where they can explore role playing and the physical sciences together. There are special areas for toddlers and parents, as well as areas for somewhat older kids. There is a child-sized neighborhood, an infant-toddlers play center, soap films and bubbles, and a children's gallery which houses exhibits on loan.

The Children's Museum also conducts workshops and special programs for parents and caregivers.

Most families drop by for one to two hours at a time. A $30 one-year family membership is available for one set of parents, all their children, and two sets of grandparents.

Seattle Center House

Seattle Center (see Chapter 8). 682-7200. Sunday through Thursday, 11–6; Friday and Saturday, 11–9. Free.

There's probably no better place in all Seattle to take children on a rainy day. Not only does it house the Seattle Children's Museum, the Piccoli Children's Theater (441-5080) (featuring puppet shows plus Winnie-the-Pooh and Mother Goose tales), but also the Seattle Center House stage presents free live performances almost daily, many of them oriented to children.

In addition, the Center contains some 25 food concessions: Mexican, Asian, pasta, salads, burgers, health foods, desserts, bakeries, and the list goes on. And there are also a dozen or more gift and novelty shops to explore.

Fun Forest

Seattle Center (see Chapter 8). 728-1585. Daily, noon to midnight through summer; hours vary rest of year; closed winter. Rides range from 75¢ to $2.25.

By any name this is an old-fashioned amusement park. There are rides for young children as well as the traditional stomach turners, and you can toss rings and throw balls for stuffed dolls just like your great-grandparents did at county fairs and traveling carnivals. To be sure, a highlight for some is a traditional merry-go-round. Even in this age of high speed, electronic zap 'em games, the old carousel retains its magic.

Gas Works Park

On Seattle's Lake Union at Northlake Way and Meridian Street. Daily, dawn to dusk. Free.

Created from the skeleton of an old gas-works plant, the antique machinery (painted and "kid-proofed") provides a magical world for youthful exploration. One of the old buildings has been recycled into a huge playbarn and picnic shed.

Gas Works Park also provides wonderful views of the boat traffic on Lake Union and of downtown Seattle. Still another attraction is its proximity to Ivar's Salmon House restaurant (just down the street), which has a takeout window for ordering chowder, fish and chips, fried clams, and other selections of Northwest soul food.

✳ Enchanted Village / Wild Waves Water Park

36201 Kit Corner Road S., Federal Way. Exit 142B from Interstate 5.
838-8828. Daily, 10–dusk, summer; closed winter. General admission $14.

This 30-acre world of fantasy really is enchanted, with a children's
petting zoo, carousel, kids' museum, aviary, putting course, snack bars,
rides, live entertainment, video games, and much, much more. It's a
spend-all-day kind of place, made to order for birthday parties—lots of
running space, picnic areas, and special activities that include live stage
performances.

Another major attraction here is the Wild Waves Park, a kids' para-
dise of water-oriented splashy fun. It includes a huge pool with artificial
ocean waves for body surfing, a water raft ride, and nine water slides of
various lengths and velocities.

✳ Aqua Barn Ranch

15227 S.E. Renton–Maple Valley Highway, Renton. 255-4618. Daily, 9–
5 (call for riding and swimming schedules). Pony rides $4.50; trail rides
$19.50 per hour. Swimming, $3.25 adults; $2.75 youths; $2.25 under 12.

With ponies, horses, and an indoor pool, this is a nice park-like center for family outings. The ranch also has camping and day camp programs for children.

The pony rides are for children of any age accompanied by a parent.
Children must be 8 or older for trail rides. There is no admission charge to
picnic at the ranch, and there are picnic tables available, ducks to feed,
and lots of bunnies. Visitor activities must dovetail with scheduled camping programs, so call ahead for schedules. There are activity packages for
groups and birthday parties.

✳ O. O. Denny Park

On Lake Washington at Holmes Point Road (turn west on Holmes Point Road
in Juanita and continue 3.5 miles to the parking lot). Free.

O.O. Denny Park boasted the tallest Douglas fir in King County
until a wind storm in January 1993 sheared the 600-year-old, 225-foot-
high giant in half. Most visitors with toddlers head immediately for the
quarter-mile beach, but trail heads across the road provide ideal routes for
introducing children to hiking on modest grades in this isolated "urban"
park.

Two infrequently traveled three-quarter-mile trails wind along Big
Finn Creek through some mixed old-growth Douglas firs and second-
growth forest in the making. One fork of the northernmost trail termi-
nates where the giant Douglas fir once stood; another leads to an overlook.

All the trails are circular one-way routes and gradual enough for the youngest little hiker to traverse.

✳ Zones

2207 N.E. Bellevue-Redmond Rd., Redmond. 746-9411. Weekdays,
11–10. Saturday, 11–midnight. Free. You pay for the games and activities.

Zones boasts more than 100 video games, along with air hockey, batting cages, and miniature golf. Love it or hate it, the video age has dawned and then some, and for rainy days, commercial video parlors may well find their place in the grand scheme, especially if you or your family accumulate quarters in large numbers. That's what video "zones" require—lots of quarters, and a tolerance for electronic sound effects.

✳ Seattle Funplex Indoor Amusement Center

1541 15th Avenue W. 285-7842. Weekdays, 11–11. Saturday, 10–1.
Free. You pay for the games and activities.

In addition to video games, miniature golf, batting cages, inflatable jungle bouncers, and go-carts, there is laser tag—a "shoot-'em-up" game of questionable social value that most kids absolutely love to play.

✳ Games Family Fun Center

3616 South Road, Mukilteo. 745-5033. Weekdays, 10–10; weekends, 10–
midnight. Free. You pay for the games and activities.

Younger children will surely enjoy whacky gator, the ball pit, and ski ball, while older kids may choose from miniature golf, batting practice, video games, air hockey, pinball machines, and pool.

✳ Funtasia

7212 220th Street S.W., Edmonds. 774-4263. Weekdays, 11–11;
Saturday, 11–2.

Here's 20,000 square feet filled with over 200 video and redemption games. "Redemption" here refers not to the personal variety, but what used to be called carnival games that you play for stuffed animals and other toys. There are bowlingo (miniature bowling), miniature golf, and neo-lighted bumper cars. An outdoor park contains batting cages, beach volleyball (you play in sand), and a splashy water-wars game.

✳ Point Defiance Park

(See Chapters 1 and 5)

Tacoma's Point Defiance Park is mentioned frequently in this guide, for many good reasons. It's a perfect destination for families with children.

To recap, the park contains swimming beaches, bathhouses, Camp Six (an outdoor logging museum), historic Fort Nisqually, Never-Never Land, and the excellent Tacoma Zoo-Aquarium complex.

With playgrounds, picnic areas, gardens, lovely views of Puget Sound, and all its other attractions, it is the region's best public park.

11

Where They Make Things

With moderate enthusiasm, children enjoy visiting factories, workshops, and studios. The point is—are they *really interesting* to children? It's a sure bet a chocolate factory is a more appropriate destination for a kid than a winery. But all kinds of manufacturing processes are fascinating when you get to look behind the scenes. A bakery, for example—magic by anyone's test.

The suggestions here are evergreens for class outings. They provide equally good family entertainment, a nice break on a long drive, or a bonus en route to a family picnic. The firms with adroit public relations staffs send visitors off with product samples, and sometimes there's an opportunity to buy products for no discount whatsoever—but it seems like a terrific deal!

Note: For every firm listed here there are dozens of others. For a child, groups of children and/or students with special interests, a phone call will often lead to a special tour arrangement. For large companies, ask for the public relations director or "whoever handles public relations." If that fails, ask for the marketing director. Although some companies have policies against visitors for reasons of safety or security, a special request may well lead to a special tour.

✵ University of Washington Marine Field Laboratories (San Juan Island)

At Friday Harbor, a mile from the ferry terminal. July and August, Wednesday and Saturday, 2–4. Free.

This is the headquarters for the University of Washington's research and marine preservation activities throughout the San Juan Islands. There are holding tanks and ponds filled with sea creatures. Guides answer questions about the marine life and studies on the 484-acre property. Scientists from around the world come here to pursue their research and educational programs, and although what you'll see and hear is never predictable, it is always fascinating.

Skagit Hydroelectric Plant

In Newhalem, operated by Seattle City Light. 684-3030. Special dinner tours, summers. Reservations required (make them early). Adults $21; Seniors $19; children (6–11) $10.

The popular four-hour tour includes an all-you-can-eat chicken barbecue. You may make reservations as early as April for the summer tours. The Skagit River scenery is beautiful along this part of the river, with moss- and fern-covered canyons, whitewater rapids, and a long, clear pool of water behind the dam. The hydroelectric machinery is explained by the tour guides, who provide an excellent introduction to how electricity is created. It's a day the entire family should enjoy.

This portion of the Skagit River watershed is so lovely and serene that many conservationists believe it would have been granted National Park status if the hydroelectric folks hadn't developed it first. North Cascades National Park is nearby.

Twin City Foods

In Stanwood, on Highway 532. 629-2111. July through September, weekdays, 8–4. Call in advance for a 30-minute tour. Free.

Possibly the biggest frozen-food packer in the world, Twin City Foods can process as much as 1.5-million pounds of peas in 24 hours! Through the summer they pack peas and corn. Maybe, just maybe, visiting the plant will convince younger children that peas are edible and not grown just for the pleasure of burying them under the mashed potatoes at dinner. On second thought…probably not. You can't fool a smart kid. The corn is OK.

Washington Cheese Factory

900 E. College Way, Mt. Vernon. 424-3510. Tuesday, Wednesday, and Friday, 9:30–5. Call first in winter. Free.

You can watch the cheese making from a viewing room here and sample caraway jack, monterey jack, cheddar, colby, and other dairy treats in a tasting room and retail store. Purchasing cheese here may not be less expensive than at your local market, but it's more fun.

Boeing Everett Plant

In Everett. Exit 189 from Interstate 5 and drive three miles west. 342-4801. Monday through Friday, 9 and 1. Children must be 10 or older. Free.

It is amazing to see just how a Boeing 747 jumbo jet is assembled. No less amazing is the size of this assembly plant; it is one of the largest buildings in the world. You travel through the plant by bus on these well-conducted guided tours.

�֎ Boehm's Candy Kitchen

255 N.E. Gilman Boulevard, Issaquah. 392-6652. Appointment required for one-hour tours, Tuesday and Friday, 10:30 and 1. Free.

First impressions to the contrary, Boehm's is not sponsored by the American Dental Association. The kitchen produces dozens of different candies, from chocolates to chews, all of them simply wonderful! Children are advised to watch their parents carefully here. Julius Boehm, who founded the factory, lived a colorful life, once serving as an Olympic Games torch carrier. A collection of his memorabilia is on display in a Swiss chalet that he built.

✖ Molbak's Greenhouse

13625 N.E. 175th, Woodinville. 454-1951. Weekdays, 8:30–4. Call four weeks in advance for guided group tours. Free.

Molbak's, a retail nursery and garden center, boasts ten acres of exotic indoor plants, garden plants, trees and shrubs, accessories, and landscape art—in all, a veritable jungle for young imaginations. The guided tours are especially nice if your knowledge of plant lore is slim, but it's fun to wander through the greenery at any time. There are always plants in bloom and some new varieties to wonder at, an aviary, and seasonal displays. The garden center also contains several specialty shops offering such treasures as bird feeders, rare gardening books, and specialty hobby items, for instance, Bonsai materials.

✖ Brenner Brothers Bakery

12000 N.E. Bellevue-Redmond Road, Bellevue. 454-0600. 30-minute tours on Wednesdays. Free.

It's a puzzle how this very urban bakery and kosher delicatessen ended up in Seattle's suburbs: Inside the atmosphere is pure New York. The informal tours introduce you to how bagels and breads are made, how cakes are frosted and decorated, and how taste buds are shamelessly teased. The bakery fragrances are devastating. Fortunately there is the adjacent delicatessen for emergency treatment of hunger pangs. The cookies available here are simply wonderful!

✖ Gilman Village

In Issaquah, via the Front Street exit. Most of the shops are open Monday through Saturday, 10–5; many are also open Sunday. Free to look.

Gilman Village is one of the growing number of shopping complexes around Puget Sound. The environment is a campus of stores, craft shops, and boutiques, small and personal in scale. The village is an assemblage of converted old houses and some new buildings designed to look venerable.

There are a variety of specialty shops and restaurants. Not all the shops are of interest to children, and some of them are unabashedly decorator cute. But it's an attractive walk around the village, and a few of the shops are irresistible to kids. There's a terrific nature store loaded with dinosaur stuff, a doll shop, Mykens, with gifts for pets and their owners, and at the Christmas House you can buy holiday items from around the world. The shopping village also contains several small restaurants, a bookstore, and another 25 or so perfume-scented boutiques.

✷ Seattle Harbor Tours

Pier 55, Seattle. 623-1445. Frequent one-hour tours, daily. Adults $11; children (5–12) $5; under 5 free. (Longer tours through the locks and around Lake Washington up to $19 adults; $9 children.)

It isn't always obvious from shore, but Seattle is a world-class seaport with many active and fascinating maritime industries. This is a tour of the Seattle waterfront, Elliott Bay, and the Duwamish waterway that should be required for every Seattle booster. You see cargo docks, ferryboats, freighters, tugs, and a surprising number of anglers who find out-of-the-way fishing spots along the shore. Views of downtown Seattle from the water are increasingly dramatic as the city's Manhattanization continues.

Seattle Harbor Tours also offers boat tours that take you through the Lake Washington Ship Canal locks and around Lake Washington, and they can accommodate private charters for groups ranging in size from 30 to 400—if your children want to invite some friends!

✷ Seattle Animal Shelter

2061 15th W., Seattle. 386-4254. Tuesday through Saturday, 12–6. Free.

This is the largest of the region's homes for unwanted pets; it is also the place where lost pets are kept until their owners claim them. It's recommended, with a couple of caveats. For one, every child is going to want to adopt a dog or cat—or all of them—and that's heartrending. And secondly, the news that pets who do not eventually find homes are destroyed is the kind of reality that can haunt a youngster...and you.

Nevertheless, it's both wonderful and amazing to see the variety of animals at the shelter, and this is certainly the place to find a pet if you are looking for one. The animals are carefully screened by veterinarians, are in excellent health, and need homes.

Scenario in one act:

MOM: We'll think about the doggy for a day or two. We don't have to decide right now.

(Two blocks away, driving in ghostly silence.)

DAD: Let's go back and get her.

CHORUS: All right!

✭ Archie McPhee & Company

3510 Stone Way N., Seattle. 545-8344. Monday through Friday, 8–6, weekends, 10–6. Free.

Commercial and zany, Archie McPhee is often described as the merchant who offers the world's largest stock of rubber critters. It's worth a visit just to pick up the mail-order catalog. The store contains thousands of novelty items, a majority of them under five dollars.

You can buy a gross of life-like rubber roaches, flamingos, banana noses, lizards that glow in the dark, slugs, dinosaurs, anatomical parts, and dolls of all descriptions—how about little rubber executives for 10 cents each or 20 for a dollar (start your own corporation!).

One popular item is a life-size rubber chicken. "You may buy only one rubber chicken in your life…why not the best?" It's that kind of reasoning that makes Archie McPhee's so irresistible.

Widely acclaimed by critics of questionable taste in such glowing terms as "Pee-Wee Herman's interior decorator" and "Der Kitsch-Kaiser," Archie McPhee's may well have no significant cultural merit whatsoever. Not to let the times pass them by, Archie McPhee recently added a new "espresso tiki hut" to the establishment, another marketing breakthrough—Rome in Polynesia!

Your children will love it and, if you'll let yourself, so will you.

✭ KIRO-TV

3rd and Broad, Seattle. 728-5085. Call Public Affairs for tour appointments, limited to groups of under ten. Free.

KIRO does an excellent job of showing visitors around. You see the combined radio and TV newsrooms, and some of KIRO's sophisticated broadcasting equipment.

✭ The Seattle Times

Fairview N. and John. 464-2285. During school year, Monday through Friday; call for an appointment. Children must be 9 or older. Free.

The *Times* is the Northwest's largest daily newspaper, and a tour of its facilities is a look at how real news is assembled and reported. No electronic flash here, just hardworking journalists putting out a good newspaper. Your tour includes the city room, editorial departments, production areas, art department, and the press room. The big printing presses are awesome. In operation they resonate with the frenetic excitement of the publishing world.

✴ University of Washington

N.E. 45th and 15th N.E., Seattle. 543-9686. Tours Monday through Friday at 2:30. Free.

Hour-long walking tours begin at 320 Schmitz Hall. The University of Washington is one of the Northwest's biggest industries and proudly boasts a magnificent campus. The tour touches upon the school's history and its educational and cultural impact upon the community. It also explores some of the campus' outstanding architecture.

Other tours are also available on campus by appointment. Of interest to children are the Kirsten Wind Tunnel (543-0439); the Fisheries Center (543-4270); special campus tours (543-9198); and the University of Washington Arboretum (543-8800).

✴ Black Diamond Bakery

In Black Diamond, State Highway 169. 886-2741. Wednesday through Friday, 8–4; weekends, 7–5. Free.

They bake bread here the old-fashioned way, in venerable brick ovens heated by alderwood fires.

Nearby you can visit the Black Diamond Historic Museum in the town's old train depot. It contains a nice exhibit of memorabilia from Black Diamond's coal mining days. Free, open weekends, 9 to 3.

✴ Seattle-Tacoma International Airport

Via Sea-Tac Airport exits from Interstate 5 and State Highway 518. 433-5386. Tours Tuesday, Wednesday, and Thursday, 9:30 and 11:30; call for appointment. Minimum group size 15. Free.

The tour includes a 15-minute slide presentation, a ride on the airport's computerized Satellite Transit System, an introduction to the security system, and a visit to the Port of Seattle Police Department. You take advantage of the airport's extensive escalator network, but this is another long walk, best for older kids.

✴ Adams Foods

1671 Lincoln, Tacoma. 272-3261. Monday through Friday. Call for appointment. Free.

Every responsible adult with a child to care for should take the youngster to a peanut butter factory. It's the American thing to do!

At Adams Foods they manufacture a delicious product, without preservatives. As good as it is—and Adams peanut butter is very good—it sticks to the roof of your mouth like all the others.

✴ Tacoma News Tribune

1950 S. State Street, Tacoma. 597-8560. Monday through Thursday, 8–2; call for appointment. Free.

One of the things that characterizes Northwest newspaper folks is their gracious friendliness, and the *Tribune* staff members are true to form. A tour of the paper includes a slide presentation and walk through the city room, art department, composing, press room, and bundling/delivery operations.

✴ Fire Boat Defiance

3301 Rustin Way, Tacoma. 591-5737. Call for appointment or take your chances on a Saturday. Free.

This is an interesting stop along scenic Rustin Way. You can go aboard the fire boat *Defiance,* explore the crew's quarters, visit the wheelhouse, and examine the water pumps and fire hose equipment. *Defiance* is a reliable attraction until there's a waterside fire...then she's off!

You can visit any of Tacoma's fire stations by appointment (591-5737). The city's firemen are among the nicest people you and your children will ever meet. They go all out to make firehouse visits informative and fun.

12

Harvesting

It's a familiar refrain: "Kids today think their food grows at Safeway." A delightful way to learn otherwise is to spend a day harvesting produce for the family table at one of the many farms in Western Washington that offer U-Pick fruits and vegetables in season.

Western Washington has an ideal climate for berries and many vegetables. The common berries are strawberries, raspberries, and blueberries. Strawberries generally ripen in early June and have a 3-week picking season. Raspberries fruit at the end of June and continue into August. Blueberries, depending on the variety, are picked from mid-July to early September. Since adults tend to over pick, make sure you have a plan for the extras which you can't eat that day, whether you cook, or can, or freeze them. U-Pick berries typically sell at 70 to 85 cents per pound, while picked berries are $1 per pound or more. Apple season ranges from mid- to late August through October. Vegetables are harvested later in the summer, during August and September.

Wear old clothes when picking fruits and vegetables. It's not a clean business. Also, bring your own containers, since not all farms provide you with something in which to take your prizes home with you. Most importantly, call first before you visit these farms, as the availability of produce is dependent on weather and how many people got there before you.

Blackberries and wild huckleberries appear in late summer. Blackberries grow like weeds. If you don't have a bush growing in your backyard already, you'll often find them in areas where original plant cover has been disturbed. In many places along Seattle's Burke-Gilman Trail you'll find these persistent berries. Pick them with care. They are thorny. Huckleberries grow along the edges of dry mountain trails and in clear cuts, usually higher in elevation. Though huckleberries look a lot like blueberries, they are much smaller, but they have a delicate, distinctive taste. With diligence, you can harvest many huckleberries in little time, and unlike blackberries, they don't bite.

If your children decide to try their own garden at home and have questions about a particular flower, fruit, or vegetable, you or they can call the Washington State University Cooperative Extension at 296-3440, weekdays from 10 to 4. Ask for the Master Gardeners and/or Master Canners. The Master Gardeners are volunteers who have taken 60 hours of agricultural training, and volunteer their time to answer questions about flowers, herbs, fruit, vegetables, and gardening in general. The Master Canners will give information about freezing, canning, pickling, jams, jellies, and food storage.

For more information on U-Pick farms and farmers' markets in nearby counties, pick up the *Farm Fresh Guide*—send a self-addressed, stamped envelope to Puget Sound Farm Markets Association, 1733 N.E. 20th Street, Renton, WA 98056 (228-9623). To get the *Farm Directory* call 252-3281 or 568-2338.

✴ Bailey Vegetables

12711 Springhetti Road, Snohomish. Three miles south of Snohomish on Springhetti Road, parallel to Highway 9. 568-8826. Mid-July to mid-October; daily, 8–8.

U-Pick potatoes, beets, pickling cucumbers, beans, zucchini, flowers (charged by the bunch) are available. Pickling cucumbers are popular since many people like to can and pickle. Flowers and fresh vegetables are also sold in season: green beans, beets, new potatoes, pickling cucumbers, and corn. Bailey Vegetables is surrounded by a dairy farm.

✴ Bakko's Berries, Etc.

7808 State Road 92, Lake Stevens. 5.5 miles east of Highway 9 on Highway 92 (Granite Falls Highway). 334-8018. Daily, 8–6:30; Sunday 10–5.

U-Pick Shuksan strawberries, Mecker raspberries, and blueberries. The blueberry season is 6 weeks, from end of July to early September. The clusters are so loaded on the blueberry bushes, you can pick over rows which have been picked before. In July and August there are U-Pick or picked kohlrabi (a type of turnip), beans, cucumbers, beets, carrots, cauliflower, broccoli, cabbage, potatoes, and picked corn. Pumpkins are available in October. If your kids' eyes are bigger than their stomachs, and you have too many berries lying around after the day's picking, you can leave strawberries in or out of the refrigerator for a maximum of 3 days, and blueberries for longer. But raspberries are best eaten, frozen, or made into jam the same day they are picked.

✴ Blueberry Farm

12109 Woods Creek Road, Monroe. Take Interstate 405 North to Woodinville; go east on Highway 2. At Red Barn Bakery turn north and drive 4 miles. At the Y in the road stay right. 794–6995. Tuesday through Saturday, 9–6; Sunday, noon–6; closed Monday.

Seven to nine varieties of blueberries, both U-Pick and picked, are available through mid-July into August at this 60-year-old farm. There are a picnic area and a play area with a castle being built. This place is like an Old McDonald's farm, with an organic garden and animals in pasture. Fresh flats of fruit, and vegetables as well, are available if you call ahead. A gift shop sells jams, honey, pottery, and handicrafts. U-Pick blueberries are 85 cents a pound.

✷ The Blueberry Patch

10410 54th Place N.E., Everett. From Interstate 5 take the Marysville exit, right into Marysville. Cross the tracks and go 3–4 miles to Highway 9. At the T intersection turn right; at .25 mile turn left (first turn) onto S. Lake Cassidy Road. At the stop sign turn left onto 54th Place N.E. Cross the bridge and go .25 mile. The house is on the right. 334-5524. Berries are available mid-July through the first week of September, or when it freezes. Daily, 8–dark.

This 2.5 acre family farm offers organically grown U-Pick and picked blueberries. Call ahead for prepicked orders. Three varieties of blueberries are available: Weymouth, Jersey, and Concord (the best and biggest). U-Pick berries are 80 cents a pound; prepicked are $1.10 a pound.

✷ Craven Farm and Pumpkin Patch

13817 Short School Road, Snohomish. In Snohomish, drive south on Lincoln Street for 3 miles; signs posted to the farm. Call to check availability. 568-2601. June through early August, daily, 8–6; October 2–31, 10–4:30.

U-Pick strawberries are available in June, raspberries from July to early August. There are other types of berries throughout the summer: marionberries, developed in Oregon, which are the closest to the black-berry in taste; tayberries, a boysenberry-raspberry cross; and sylvans, a boysenberry-marionberry cross. Jams, syrups, and honey are available in the gift shop; the jam is certified organic. The Pumpkin Patch is open October 2–31, and at $3.50 per child (adults free) includes story time (with a cookie), scarecrow making, and a trip to the pumpkin field where each child can find a special Halloween pumpkin and sweet corn, gourds, and squash.

✷ Green's Acres Blueberry Farm

32326 132nd Street S.E., Sultan. 793-1714. Daily, 9–dusk.

Whether they are Early Blues, Blue Rays, Blue Crops, Berkeleys, or Elizabeths, blueberries are available from early July to September here, both U-Pick and prepicked. Kids are given a "neck bucket" and 4–5 gallon buckets to put the berries in as they go. Berries are 75 cents a pound

U-Pick, $1 a pound picked. Every year the owners publish a brochure
with blueberry recipes, including their favorite recipe of the year. If kids
get tired of picking, they can always throw sticks for Georgia, the farm's
blueberry expert, a black Labrador retriever.

✴ Golden Gardens
*On the western shore of Ballard, Seattle. In Ballard, take Market Street west
to Seaview N.W.; follow road to end into Golden Gardens Park. Closes at
dusk. Free.*

Between the parking lot and the beach there is a huge clump of
blackberry bushes which flourish in the August sun. You can take your
kids there time and time again because the blackberries don't ripen at the
same time. These bushes are big and have thorns, so be sure your kids
wear heavy clothing covering their arms and legs.

✴ Hagen Vegetables
*8203 Marsh Road, Snohomish. Exit 186 from Interstate 5. Five miles east,
midway between Highway 9 and the bottom of Seattle Hill Road (Larimer's
corner). 668-8588. Open to October 31, Monday through Saturday, 9–7;
Sunday, 11–7.*

U-Pick green beans, cucumbers, peas, pumpkins, and U-Cut flowers
are available. The farm stand offers picked beets, broccoli, cabbage, carrots, cauliflower, corn, cucumbers, dill, garlic, lettuce, potatoes, winter
squash, zucchini, leeks, turnips, onions, brussels sprouts, tomatoes, kohlrabi. Free hay rides are given in October during pumpkin season. Between
70 and 80 different vegetables are grown here.

✴ Harvold Berry Farm
*32325 N.E. 55th, Carnation. North of city limits on Highway 203 (the
Carnation-Duvall Road). 333-4185. June through mid-August, daily, 8–8.*

U-Pick Shuksan strawberries mid-June to mid-July, and raspberries
July to mid-August. Free containers are provided.

✴ The Herbfarm
*32804 Issaquah–Fall City Road, Fall City. 784-2222. Daily, 9–5.
Restaurant open April through January only (reservations required).*

The Herbfarm, with 639 different herbs in 17 different herb gardens,
will host groups (minimum 10 children and 5 adults) on free tours of the
display gardens and potted herbs. Children can learn about all the different types of herbs available and what they are used for. The gardens are

open from late May to early September. For adults there is a gift shop, and cooking, gardening, and craft classes. There is one class for children, "A Child's Garden," which offers children ages 8 to 12 hands-on experience in planting their own gardens. The restaurant chefs use many of the farm's products in their recipes.

✳ Laura & Bob Johnson

5211 52nd Street S.E., Everett. Three miles from Everett. Take Exit 194 off Interstate 5 (or Hewitt Avenue from Everett). Take the first right turn past a trestle onto Home Acres Road. Follow the paved road for 2.5 miles. At the bridge bear left, down the lane to the stand. 252-3281. July through October, daily, 9–6.

Sold at the stand or available for U-Pick are raspberries, basil, dill, beans, beets, pickling cucumbers, yellow and white corn, corn stalks, gourds, and squash. A Pumpkin Patch ($3 per child) is open during the last 3 weeks of October, when kids take a wagon ride to the patch to choose their favorite pumpkin (reservations needed on weekends). There are picnic tables and also farm animals to see.

✳ Kennydale Blueberry Farm

1733 N.E. 20th Street, Renton. Exit 6 from Interstate 405, on the east side of the freeway. Follow fence around school; turn right onto N.E. 28th, then left onto Jones Avenue, then 8 blocks to N.E. 20th. Turn left and look for third house on the left. 228-9623. Mid-July through late September, Monday through Saturday, 8–7; closed Sunday.

Both picked and U-Pick blueberries are available. Call in advance if you want 10 pounds or more of picked berries.

✳ Kurt's Produce

17819 Highway 203, Monroe. In Monroe, at Lewis and Main intersection, head south on Lewis for .75 mile. The farm is on the left. 794-5940. Daily, 9–6.

It's Russian Roulette over the U-Pick produce at this farm, so come out and see what's ready for you to pick and what's not: Strawberries in June; raspberries and peas in July; flowers and herbs (basil, cilantro, parsley) through September; garlic in August and September; beans, cucumbers, and dill in August; cauliflower, broccoli, cabbage, and zucchini from mid-July to November; corn and potatoes from August to November; squash and pumpkins from September to November. Everything is available U-Pick and at the farm stand. For large quantities, call first. Precut Christmas trees are available in December.

�֍ Lydon's Blueberry Farm

14510 Kelly Road N.E., Duvall. Going into Duvall, take the first left after the bridge. This road angles to the right. After 5 miles bear right at the Y in the road, onto Kelly Road. After 1 mile, the farm is on the left. 788-1395. Mid-July until frost, Wednesday through Sunday, 9–dusk; closed Monday and Tuesday.

Weymouth blueberries are sold at the farm stand or U-Pick. The farm provides coffee cans to pick with. The kids might discover the fish pond and swing set next to the fields.

✖ Merv's U-Pick Berry Farm

17614 Highway 203, Monroe. One-half mile south of Monroe on Monroe-Duvall Highway. 794-8080. June and August, daily, 8–dusk unless picked out.

Harvest your own strawberries through July, and pick raspberries from late June through late July or early August. If you're lucky you can see the barn owl that frequents the place.

✖ Mountainview Tree Forest

29231 132nd Avenue S.E., Auburn. One and one-quarter miles south of Highway 516 (Kent-Langley Road) on 132nd Avenue S.E. Or go 1.25 miles north of Highway 18 on 132nd Avenue at the Green River Community College exit. 631-0139. From the Friday after Thanksgiving to December 24, daily, 9–8.

This farm has a wide variety of U-Cut Christmas trees from which to select, including Noble, Fraser, Grand, and Douglas firs; Blue and Green spruces; and Sequoias. A saw and a map are provided, and with these handy items you can find the tree of your child's dreams. Douglas firs are a minimum of $21 a tree, any size, and the Nobles and Frasers are a minimum of $38 a tree, any size. If you don't want to cut your own, you can purchase a precut Douglas fir. Every hour on the hour there is a free tractor-drawn hayride for the kids. At the gift shop you can buy flocked trees (sprayed with "snow"), swags, wreaths, poinsettias, bows, tree ornaments, and crafts. And when you get tired of tree chopping, there is an espresso bar for you and candy canes for the kids.

✖ Overlake Blueberry Farm

2380 Bellevue Way S.E., Bellevue. 454-3539. Early July to mid-September; October 15–31; Monday through Friday, 8–6; Saturday 8–5; closed Sunday.

This farm offers U-Pick Concord blueberries and pumpkins as well as prepicked raspberries, strawberries, tomatoes, peaches, and pears. At the stand there are a host of blueberry specialties, including pies, syrup, dried blueberries, blueberry recipes, and more. During October the farm provides children with paints and materials to color pumpkins and make scarecrows. There is also a wetlands farm tour on Tuesdays and Thursdays at 10 for smaller family groups. (Call ahead for an appointment for larger school groups.) For $1 a person, children can learn about wetlands and wetland plants. A grassy picnic area can be reserved for birthday parties and special events.

✼ Remlinger Farms

32610 N.E. 32nd Street, Carnation. 451-8740 or 333-4135. One mile south of Carnation on Highway 203. April through December.

Here you'll find U-Pick and ready-picked berries (blueberries, cherries, raspberries, rhubarb, strawberries) and other crops, in addition to a large produce store, nursery, restaurant (lunch only), bakery, barnyard animal petting area, and seasonal festivals. Remlinger Farms is famous for its fresh-frozen U-Bake homemade berry pies of every imaginable type, including loganberry, marionberry, bluegoose, and bumbleberry. Children's pony rides are given for $2, and covered-wagon rides for $1. Throughout the summer, Tuesdays are Children's Days.

"My Day on the Farm" is an all-day class tour ($15 per child), consisting of a 2-hour presentation on plants, farm animals, and ponies—complete with a pony ride. In the fall, catch the Harvest Tour ($5 per person), which offers information on a variety of farm topics, an Indian Village, a "Trapper Cabin," a Pioneer House, and a Pumpkin Patch. In December you can cut your own Christmas tree. A Party Barn can be rented for birthdays and special events.

✼ Russell Blueberry Farm

3707 122nd Street N.E., Marysville. Exit 202 off Interstate 5, east on 116th Street N.E. to Smokey Point Boulevard. Take first road to left on 122nd Street N.E. The farm is three blocks, on the right. 653-9490. Call first, as hours vary, but generally 8–8, Friday; 9–5 Saturday and Sunday.

Eight varieties of U-Pick blueberries are available from mid-July through the end of August.

✼ Serres Farm

20306 N.E. 50th Street, Redmond. 868-3017. Three miles east of Redmond on State Road 202 (Redmond–Fall City Highway). At a gray barn, turn right (south) on Sahalee Way. After one block (.15 mile), turn right (west) for .25 mile on 50th Street to the farm. June to mid-July, daily, 8–8.

U-Pick Shuksan and Cascade strawberries. Cardboard boxes and trays are provided.

✳ Snow's Berry Farm

18401 Tualco Road, Monroe. From Monroe head one mile south on Highway 203 (Duvall Highway); turn right onto Tualco Road and watch for the sign on the left. 794-6312. Daily, 7–7.

Call ahead for U-Pick and prepicked orders of Shuksan and Rainier strawberries and raspberries through July. This is a "Centennial Farm," part of an original land grant of 168 acres dating from the 1860s. After 5 generations, the farm is still in the family.

✳ Stockers "The Corn King"

10622 Airport Way, Snohomish. One-half mile south of Harvey's Airport, near Highway 9 and Marsh Road crossing. 568-2338. Roadside stand open daily, 9–dusk, spring until mid-summer. Restaurant open 11–7.

At Stockers you'll find U-Pick beans, cucumbers, and pumpkins as well as sweet corn, beets, broccoli, cabbage, cauliflower, carrots, peas, summer and winter squash, corn stalks, peaches, apples, and more. Local milk, eggs, and honey are sold. The "kiddy's barnyard" has ducks, chickens, geese, rabbits, goats, and pigs; children can see little chicks being born from incubated eggs. The restaurant on the farm, M&J Barbecue, serves sandwiches and Southern barbecued beef, ribs, and chicken.

✳ Sunset Orchards and Herbs

17425 Sunset Road, Bothell. Interstate 405 to Bothell-Everett Highway, then take the 164th Mill Creek exit. Go south 1.5–2 miles to 180th. Go east on 180th; turn left onto Sunset Road and after .5 mile turn left again into Sunset Orchards. 481-0777. April through December, Thursday through Sunday, 12–5. Closed on major holidays and 2 weeks in late August.

Pick your own apples (Red Delicious, Golden Delicious, King, McIntosh) in late summer and fall. On weekends in October and November, kids get a lecture on apples and bees, and watch cider being made ($3 a child). They see apples squeezed into juice with an old-time press, and are given sacks to collect different varieties of apples. Fresh cider and applesauce are available every morning. Kids can also observe beehives behind a protective screen, and walk around a display garden with potted culinary herbs. Potted herbs start in April; other spices June through November.

✳ Susie's Produce

43311 196th Avenue S.E., Enumclaw, on corner of Auburn-Enumclaw Highway and 196th. 825-7429. April through October, daily, 10–7.

U-Pick fruits and vegetables are strawberries, raspberries, beans, beets, broccoli, carrots, corn, zucchini, lettuce, squash, pickling cucumbers, dill, tomatoes, pumpkins, and gourds. Also available are prepicked asparagus, blueberries, cauliflower, cabbage, celery, peppers, potatoes, onions, garlic, melons, eggs, and honey.

✴ Terry's Berries at Larson Lake

700 148th Avenue S.E., Bellevue. Take Intersate 90 east to Exit 11B and go 1.4 miles north to the intersection of 8th and 148th. 641-1939. Early July to mid-September, daily, 9–6; closed Sunday.

Eight varieties of U-Pick blueberries are available. (The best time for blueberries here is in August.) Prepicked blackberries, strawberries, raspberries, and blueberries are also sold. The farm is surrounded by Bellevue City Park, which has a fish pond and walking trails; one trail crosses the blueberry fields.

13

Special Events

The Puget Sound region has more than its share of special events, many of them perfect for children. With their animals, carnivals, entertainments, and many other attractions, fairs are especially well suited to the interests of youngsters.

Big is not necessarily better when it comes to kids. For example, the annual Western Washington Fair in Puyallup may be the grandest country fair in the area each year, but the smaller Evergreen Fair in Monroe is a better choice for young children. There seem to be more young kids (4-H and Future Farmers) participating in the Evergreen Fair, and walking distances are not so great as on the Puyallup Fair Grounds.

Similarly, some of the small street fairs are better choices for children than, say, the annual Pacific Northwest Arts and Crafts Fair in Bellevue, which is terrific in its fashion, but also big, crowded, and commercial.

Characteristic of many of Western Washington's special events is an abundance of food for sale. If it's an event, the food and drink vendors appear in droves. It's politic to be prepared to buy some edibles.

Numbers are provided to confirm dates, times, and admissions (these are sometimes moving targets). To receive a copy of Washington's very useful statewide planning guide, *Destination Washington*, write: Washington State Department of Trade & Economic Development, Tourism Development Division, 101 General Administration Building, Olympia, WA 98504-0613.

Many of these events are in King County, and information will be available from the East King County Convention and Visitors Bureau (455-1926). Information for various community events will be available from local chambers of commerce listed in the yellow pages.

❖ April

Daffodil Festival, Puyallup; 627-6176

Skagit Valley Tulip Festival; 428-8547

Just for Kids Children's Festival, Olympia; 754-8017

Rock & Gem Show, Bellingham; 734-7138

Washington Hunter & Jumper Spring Nationals, Monroe; 794-7832

Norwegian Heritage Festival, Tacoma; 535-7532

❖ May

Snohomish Historical Society Annual Vaudeville Show, Snohomish; 568-2526

Opening Day of Yachting Season, Port Orchard; 876-3505

Historic Homes Tour, Port Townsend; 385-2722

Wooden Boat Festival, Olympia; 943-5404

Norwegian Constitution Day, Seattle; 543-0645

Viking Fest, Poulsbo; 779-4848

University District Street Fair, Seattle; 527-2567

Ski to Sea Festival, Bellingham; 734-1330

Northwest Folklife Festival, Seattle; 684-7300

❖ June

Salty Sea Days, Everett; 339-1113

All Citywide Garage Sale, Edmonds; 776-6711

Highland Games, Ferndale; 734-9199

Dino Daze, Olympia; 786-5595

Greek Festival, Seattle; 323-8557

Philippine Festival, Seattle; 684-7200

Pioneer Rodeo, Roy; 843-1113

Strawberry Festival, Marysville; 659-7664

Fairwood Arts & Crafts Fair, Renton; 235-9777

Strawberry Festival, Poulsbo; 779-5209

Fremont District Street Fair, Seattle; 633-4409

Ezra Meeker Community Festival, Puyallup; 848-1770

Fathoms O' Fun, Port Orchard; 876-3505

Heritage and Strawberry Festival, Burien; 244-7808

Snoqualmie Railroad Days, Snoqualmie; 888-4440

Loggerodeo, Sedro-Woolley; 855-1841

Fourth of July Frontier Days, Arlington; 435-3708

❖ July

Choochokam Festival of the Arts, Langley; 221-7494

Lynn-O-Rama, Lynnwood; 776-2147

Old Fashioned Fourth of July Celebration, Edmonds, 776-6711

Freedom Festival of Snohomish County, Everett; 259-0300

Down-Home Time Fourth of July Picnic, Issaquah; 392-0661

Fratelli's Fireworks Festival, Seattle; 622-5123

Bon Odori, Seattle; 329-0800

Lake Union Wooden Boat Festival; 382-2628

Public Pyrotechnic Display for the Centennial, Port Townsend; 385-0163

Northwest Trek Slug Festival, Eatonville; 832-6116

Taste of Tacoma, Tacoma; 232-2982

Northwest Drum & Bugle Corps Competition (Liberty Cup), Edmonds; 776-6711

Experimental Aircraft Association Fly-In, Arlington; 435-5857

Capital Lakefair, Olympia; 934-7344

West Seattle Street Fair, Seattle; 935-0904

Bear Festival, McCleary; 495-3666

SeaFair, Seattle; 728-0123

SeaFair U.S. West Milk Carton Derby, Seattle; 728-0123

Lakefair Bed Races, Olympia; 786-5595

Discovery Days at Birch Bay, Birch Bay; 371-7675

King County Fair, Enumclaw; 825-7777

Oregon Trail Days, Tenino; 264-5075

Prairie Day, Yelm; 458-3492

Pacific Northwest Arts and Crafts Fair, Bellevue; 454-4900

The Original Elma Slug Festival, Elma; 482-2212

Waterland Festival, Des Moines; 878-7000

Camlann Medieval Faire, Carnation; 788-1353

McChord Air Show, McChord AFB; 984-5637

Annual Pacific Northwest Highland Games, Enumclaw; 522-2874

Salmon Derby, Port Townsend; 385-4339

Arts & Action, Port Angeles; 457-8604

Celebrate Olympia—A Family Festival, Olympia; 753-8380

❖ August

SeaFair Torchlight Parade, Seattle; 728-0123

SeaFair Budweiser Cup Hydroplane Race, Seattle; 728-0123

Camlann Medieval Faire, Carnation; 788-1353

Lake City Salmon Bake, Lake City; 362-4378

Old Time New Age Chautauqua, Port Townsend; 624-4415

Bubble Festival, Seattle; 443-2001

SeaFair Nationals, Kent; 631-1550

U.S. Navy Blue Angels SeaFair Airshow, Seattle; 728-0123

Evergreen Classic Benefit Horse Show, Redmond; 329-9490

Grays Harbor County Fair, Elma; 482-2651

Skagit County Fair, Mount Vernon; 336-2332

Jefferson County Fair, Port Townsend; 385-3139

Taste of Edmonds, Edmonds; 776-6711

Clallam County Fair, Port Angeles; 457-7315

Canterbury Faire & Hot Air Balloon Classic, Kent; 859-3991

Good Ole Union Days, Union; 898-2310

International Air Fair, Everett; 355-2266

San Juan County Fair, Friday Harbor; 378-5240

Kitsap County Fair, Bremerton; 895-3895

Port Angeles Derby Days, Port Angeles; 452-4404

Evergreen State Fair, Monroe; 794-7832

Pet Parade, Olympia; 754-5441

Junior Rodeo Finals, Enumclaw; 825-7777

Flower Show, Seattle; 659-1450

Fun Run Parade & Fair Days' Parade, Monroe; 794-5488

❖ September

Evergreen State Fair, Monroe; 794-7832

Bumbershoot, The Seattle Arts Festival, Seattle; 622-5123

Labor Day Children's Parade, Grayland; 267-7872

Seafood Festival, Westport; 1-800-345-6223

Junior Rodeo Day, Sumas; 988-2277

Salmon Derby, Port Angeles; 457-4971

Derby Days Arts & Crafts, Port Angeles; 457-8604

Farmers Market, Puyallup; 845-6755

Pioneer Rodeo, Roy; 843-1113

Annual Port Townsend Wooden Boat Festival, Port Townsend; 385-3628

Western Washington Fair, Puyallup; 845-1771

Fairwood Arts & Crafts Fair, Renton; 235-9777

Peninsula Dog Fancier's Show, Bremerton; 692-2190

Salmon Days Walk, Issaquah; 392-0661

National Children's Day Celebration, Olympia; 753-8380

October

Toy and Doll Show, Redmond; 885-3684

Candlelight Tours of Fort Nisqually, Tacoma; 591-5339

Sausage Fest, Everett; 252-4093

Model Railroad Show, Lynden; 354-5995

Salmon Day, Issaquah; 392-0661

Hickory Shirt & Mushroom Festival, Forks; 374-6505

Octoberfest & Halloween Party, Edmonds; 776-6711

Monster Manor, Langley; 321-6799

Underwater Pumpkin Carving & Costume Party, Edmonds; 771-6322

Halloween Parade & Festivities, Tenino; 786-5595

Goblin Splash, Everett; 259-0300

Children's Halloween Night, Olympia; 753-8380

Index